We take pleasure in supplying you with a review
copy of
I CRY WHEN THE SUN GOES DOWN:
The Story of Herman Wrice

by   Jean Horton Berg

PUBLICATION DATE   October 20, 1975

PRICE $6.95

We shall appreciate receiving two copies of
your printed or typewritten review. Ad-
dress Advertising Department, Witherspoon
Building, Philadelphia, Pa. 19107. Thank you.

THE WESTMINSTER PRESS

Witherspoon Building Philadelphia, Pa. 19107

I CRY WHEN
THE SUN GOES DOWN

WESTMINSTER PRESS BOOKS
BY JEAN HORTON BERG

I Cry When the Sun Goes Down—
The Story of Herman Wrice

What Harry Found When He Lost Archie

Nobody Scares a Porcupine

Miss Tessie Tate

Miss Kirby's Room

There's Nothing to Do, So Let Me Be You

I CRY
WHEN
THE SUN
GOES DOWN,

THE STORY OF
HERMAN WRICE

by Jean Horton Berg

1975

THE WESTMINSTER PRESS · PHILADELPHIA

BOOK DESIGN BY DOROTHY E. JONES

PUBLISHED BY THE WESTMINSTER PRESS ®
PHILADELPHIA, PENNSYLVANIA

PRINTED IN THE UNITED STATES OF AMERICA

PICTURE CREDITS

Brown and Goldfarb Architects: pp. 83, 87, 147
Emery Jeffreys III: pp. 21, 29, 32
Frank Ross: p. 6
University of Pennsylvania: pp. 137, 143, 150
Villanova University: p. 150

Library of Congress Cataloging in Publication Data

Berg, Jean Horton.
  I cry when the sun goes down.

  Includes index.
  SUMMARY: A biography of a founder of the Young Great Society, an organization in Philadelphia which directs such cooperative community activities as day care, drug counseling, job training, and housing.
  1. Wrice, Herman—Juvenile literature. 2. Young Great Society—History—Juvenile literature. [1. Wrice, Herman. 2. Young Great Society—History. 3. Negroes—Biography] I. Title.
HV99.P5B47   362'.062'74811   [92]   75-20387
ISBN 0-664-32570-X

To
Those of all ages and in all ages
who truly believe in
the Brotherhood of Man

Herman's "family," 1975: *Bottom*—Toby, Timmy (and Bingo), John, Keith (arm around John). *Second row*—Terry, Tyrone, Jimmy. *Top row*—Tony, Mrs. McGriff (holding Domica), Tammy, Jean, Hattie Thompson

Introduction

A few years ago I began reading news stories and feature articles in the Philadelphia newspapers about an organization called The Young Great Society and its youthful president, Herman Wrice. Although I mentally applauded the group and its leader, I never expected to know them at firsthand. Then one day I came upon several paragraphs describing Herman's work with delinquent boys. The brief article mentioned "the twenty-eight-year-old Wrice, his wife, and their seventeen children."

"Twenty-eight years old, and seventeen children!" I exclaimed. "This man must be like the old woman that lived in a shoe. I've got to meet him."

I hurried to make an appointment to meet Herman Wrice. I wanted to interview him and write a feature article about him for *The Christian Science Monitor*. Which I did.

I met Herman; his wife, Jean; his mother, Hattie Thompson; his sister, Delores; and six of the seventeen children. These six were born to Herman and Jean. The other eleven were teen-agers who had been in trouble with the law and whom the courts had awarded to Herman and Jean as foster children. Some of these boys I came to know later, and I appreciated the fact that they enjoyed the same privileges and disciplines in the Wrice home that those born in that home had. I also met dozens of men and women connected with The Young Great Society.

The more I learned about this organization and its work, the more I admired its courage and its goals. I knew that there had to be a central force keeping it going, and that Herman Wrice was that force. And so I determined to find out as much as I could about him —where he came from and how he became the man that he is.

This is the story of one small boy who managed to break through barriers and climb over obstacles until, grown to manhood, he began wrestling with the greatest challenge of his life.

[1]

Hugging his knees to his chest, the small boy huddled on the ground under the wooden steps. His brown eyes sparkled and a mischievous grin flickered across his face at the sound of his grandmother's voice: "Herman! Herman! Now where'd that boy get to?"

Herman held his breath as Hattie Overton walked across the porch, her step light but firm over his head.

She called again. Her voice sounded cross. "He knows it's time to go," she said loudly. "Well, nothin' to do but go on 'thout him."

A clinking sound told Herman his grandmother had picked up the galvanized buckets beside the door. Now she was starting down the steps, her feet tapping the worn treads smartly.

"Dog-*gone*. She's really goin' 'thout me!" Herman peered out from his hiding place. His grandmother was twenty feet from the house and moving fast. "Momma! *Momma!* Wait up. I'm comin'."

Hattie didn't turn around or show any sign that she heard him. But she stooped to ease her heel into her flat shoe with one finger.

Her grandson caught up with her just as she straightened up and started off again.

"You didn't wait," he said reproachfully. "An' I kep' hollerin' at you, too."

"*You* didn't come, an' I kep' callin' *you*." Her tone was conversational.

"Kep' callin' me!" Herman was scornful. "One little ol' bitty time you called. An' that's all."

His grandmother's eyes flashed. "Oh, you did hear me, then. You know I called you once. How come you didn't see fit to answer? How many times you expec' to be called before you answer?"

Herman took the empty pails from her. "I was under the steps keepin' cool," he said. "I was sittin' there just as quiet. I was waitin' for you to look for me. I heard your shoes *spwack-spwack-spwackin'* down the steps. An' I was waitin' for you to look for me. I was right there all the time."

"Looka here, child." Hattie slowed her pace to accommodate the boy's. "When I call I expec' you to come. I'm callin' for a reason. I'm not callin' because I like to hear my own voice. Now come on. The ladies will be waitin' for us."

Herman's eyes swept up to steal a quick look at his grandmother's calm face. Satisfied that she wasn't really cross, he skipped over to the side of the road and snatched a blade of sweet grass to chew on.

The ladies of Crites were indeed waiting for them. Divided into groups according to their separate conversations, they crowded around the pump when Herman and his grandmother approached.

"You're late," called one. "I thought we was goin' to have the pump to ourselves today."

"I thought maybe you wan't comin' at all," cackled Mrs. Smith. Her glassy yellow-brown eyes and the way she cocked her head when she talked always made Herman think of the chickens in their little pens on the West Virginia hillside.

"Well, you see, I couldn't get this boy goin'." Hattie Overton laughed her deep rich laugh. "So I'm a little bit late. But you know I *got* to come to the pump.

10

How'm I gonna cook? How'm I gonna wash? How'm I gonna scrub my porch if I don't have any water? While you were so busy thinkin', did you think about that, Sally?"

"Hat Overton, my back's still bad." A small stooped woman tugged at Hattie's arm to get her attention. "You hear? I say my back's still bad."

"Did you try puttin' a board under your mattress, Miss Clara?" Hattie asked.

"Why, no, I ditn'," Miss Clara said. "But I will. Thank you, Hat Overton. Thank you kindly."

"Come on, Herman." Hattie reached for the pails the boy was carrying. "Get to work, now."

Herman didn't have to be called twice this time. Mrs. Patton, who lived closest to the town pump and regularly supplied the priming water, poured it in. But Herman was already pumping the old iron handle up and down, jumping to keep his hold on it as it swung up and hanging his full weight on it to bring it down.

The pump squealed loudly and hiccuped with each sudden outflow. Then it settled into spewing forth a steady stream of cool water, accompanied by a quavering complaint.

This was the highlight of most days for Herman. While the older children, including his sister, Delores, were in school, there was very little for him to do. He didn't like playing with children his own age.

"They only want to do baby things," he complained when his grandmother urged him to play with this child or that one.

The daily trip to the pump gave Herman a sense of being where the action was. Manning the pump gave him the feeling of being in control of things—a feeling that was becoming more and more necessary to him.

Each one of the twenty-five company houses making up the mining village was exactly like the other twenty-four. The gray frame boxes perched awkwardly on cement-block pillars to escape the regular flooding of the creek.

The seven small rooms in each house did not include a bathroom. (The necessary room was just behind the house.) Nor was there running water in the kitchens. All water, for whatever purpose, had to be carried from the town pump.

Three almost-mountains joined to form what was for some of the villagers a shelter, for others a prison. Herman saw them as foreboding prison walls, with the sky above the village as the lone window through which he could look. One coal train and one passenger train rolled slowly through town each day, testifying that a world existed beyond the mountains.

After he learned to count, Herman found some small excitement in counting the cars of the trains as they passed.

Besides the two-room school where his sister went, the big school, the company houses, one store, one church, one creek, one bridge over the creek, and four coal mines made up Crites—population ninety souls.

Because there were no village lights, bedtime for everyone, young and old, was seven o'clock. Four in the morning was rising time.

A certain fixed social system, including regularly performed routine, evolved from the village's limited physical and mental dimensions as well as from its benefactor and master—Coal. Early in the morning, after their men left for the mines, the women gathered at the pump not only to fill their pails with water to fight the dust and grime which were King Coal's trademark but to visit, gossip, and share ideas.

Hattie Overton was the acknowledged leader of these women. She played the roles of philosopher, physician, nurse, and mother. Along with providing a willing pumper in Herman, she dispensed advice when it was asked for and mediated quarrels. Her

Snapshots taken in Crites, W. Va., of persons important to Herman, *clockwise from upper left:* Delores and Hattie with Herman and a playmate in front of company houses; Delores with her prized possession; young Hattie— Herman's mother; Grandmother Hattie

grandson's pride in her came second only to his love for her.

He couldn't remember when he and Delores had first come to live with their grandparents, but he had heard the story often enough. Tall, lean Charlie Wrice, a city boy from Birmingham, Alabama, had courted the Overtons' daughter (another Hattie), and won her soon after her sixteenth birthday. During a period when he was out of work, Charlie brought his little family back to Crites and persuaded his father-in-law to help him get a job in the coal mines.

Presumably Harvey Overton was happy about the whole thing. It was hard to tell. Unless something displeased him, he was uncommunicative, never wasting a word when a grunt or a gesture would do. His wife was plainly delighted to have her daughter back, and she loved her grandchildren dearly. When Charlie went off to war upon the draft board's invitation, she offered no objection to her daughter's going to Indianapolis to work in a defense plant.

"You go along," she said, "an' earn the money. The babies will be just fine with me."

And they were. They thrived on their grandmother's strength and care. Delores' memories of her parents drifted to the back of her thinking, hidden from view by the present reality of Hattie and Harvey Overton. She soon found playmates her own age and enjoyed their companionship. She was a bright little girl who, without seeming to strive for it, became the leader of whatever group she joined. Her days in the two-room school were productive and happy. She had the gift of making her environment do what she wanted it to do and appear to be what she wanted it to be. At home she did the simple chores her grandmother required of her and helped with the little brother, whom she truly loved. If she missed her parents, she gave no sign of it.

Herman had no recollection of his parents. To him

14

they were people his grandparents talked about. When Harvey Overton turned on the big Zenith radio after supper, he paid particular attention to the newscasts interrupting *Fibber McGee and Molly* and *Beulah.* With both his son, Sam, and Charlie Wrice in the Pacific theater of war, Harvey listened anxiously for whatever word he could get from that area.

"Fightin', fightin'," he muttered one night. "Makes you wonder what's so important to do all that fightin' about. What's so important to kill all the men for? Why can't they just stop fightin'?"

Herman wondered if fighting in the Pacific was anything like fighting at home. When his grandfather uncoiled his six feet five inches from the old chair he called his special chair and headed toward the door, Hattie made no effort to hide her feelings. "You goin' out drinkin' tonight, Harvey Overton?"

"I thought I'd maybe have a drink with the fellows." Harvey's answer always came on a defensive note.

And then there were words—hot words of reproach and resentment calling forth hotter words. Harvey soon got around to telling in words of one syllable how he felt about the crosses, Biblical pictures, and religious mottoes Hattie kept "plastering all over the house." Actually, she put them on the walls only in her bedroom, but to the outraged Harvey they appeared to spoil every room. Sometimes the heat died down quickly. Sometimes it lasted awhile. But whatever happened, Harvey never stopped going out to have a drink with the fellows.

The mountains, although they stood between him and freedom, provided Herman and the rest of the village with some necessities as well as some pleasure. On the lower, ledgelike slopes, safely above flood level, every family had a pen with some pigs in it. And every family had a pen with some chickens. At a little dis-

15

tance above the pens, each family had a small garden where they grew enough vegetables for their own immediate needs.

A part of the routine of the village was the caring for this hillside of eatables.

In the summertime, as soon as his grandmother finished her compulsive scrubbing of the porch—bleached white through her daily efforts—Herman began teasing her to go to the garden.

"C'mon, Momma, we got to go pull weeds. An' maybe the carrots are ready. C'mon," he would coax, all the while dancing around on his toes, ready to be off at the first sign Hattie was coming.

Only when he was climbing the side of the mountain did Herman feel free. Only then did he know for sure that someday he would leave the prison and enter the wide world beyond the barrier.

Sometimes Hattie was ready to go. Sometimes she held him back with, "You mostly want to pull weeds before we get there. I don't notice you doin' much about them when we're actually there. You're lazy, that's what."

This last wasn't quite true. Because Herman always wanted to be doing something. From the time he could walk, his biggest enemy was inactivity. He may not have done much weeding, but that was because he would have found something more exciting to do. Stooping in one spot to pull weeds wasn't his idea of action.

Except for Tuesdays, Thursdays, and Sundays, Hattie allowed her grandson to coax her up the hillside. Usually she carried Herman on her back, walking briskly, sometimes even running up the steep slopes like a girl. ("No sense goin' slow when the walkin's hard.") She was apt to pry rocks loose with the handle of the mallet she always carried and let them roll

16

noisily down into the valley. ("We don' want to trip on 'em or slip on 'em.")

One day Herman was scrambling up ahead of her. A whirring in the grass ahead stopped him. "It's a big grasshopper, Momma," he cried. "Lemme catch him an' make him spit tobacco."

In one electric instant Hattie swept the boy behind her as she aimed the head of the mallet. Peeking out from behind her skirts, the startled child saw a rattlesnake thrashing wildly in a fruitless effort to release its head pinned firmly to the ground by the mallet.

Hattie leaned hard on the handle and didn't straighten up until the snake had lain quiet for a long time. "Don' you touch it," she warned when Herman would have gone close. "A snake don' die till the sun goes down. We'll come back tomorrow an' cut off his rattles. An' don' ever—not *ever* come up here by yourself. You hear?"

"Some grasshopper," Harvey grunted when he heard about the excitement. Which was the most he had said to anyone in the family since the last discussion he had had with Hattie about the possibility of his going to church—where she spent most of Sunday—or about letting her keep the Zenith tuned in to the Nashville station that blared out the gospels.

At quarter to five on every workday afternoon a basin of pump water was hot and ready for Harvey to wash in when he came home from the mine. Water was ready for the man of every house to make himself presentable for the supper, which was always served promptly at five. No woman worth her salt would embarrass her husband by tampering with this sacred schedule.

Harvey came out into the daylight along with the rest of the men at a little after four. They were a club whose membership included every able-bodied male in the village. Aching and creaking and indistinguishable in their coal-dust masks, they sat on the bridge washing off the worst of the grime before they went home. As they washed, they talked.

"What do you think of the new foreman?"

"I gotta get me a new lamp."

"I heard someone up to the store talkin' strike."

"What'll you do if it comes?"

Communication among the men was unlabored and unhampered. And why not? They worked together. They respected one another. And every man's safety depended on each one's doing his job right. From four in the morning until quitting time there was no difference among them. When they came out of the mine at the end of the day, and sat on the bridge over the creek to wash, you could see who was black and who was white. But that didn't make any difference to them. They did the same work for the same pay, and they depended on one another for their very lives. There was no segregation in the mines.

Differences in skin color had no importance to Herman until he ran over to Susie's house one Friday afternoon to ask her to play ball with him. Susie was a special friend of Delores and often spent the night at Overtons'.

Herman stood at the bottom of the steps and called excitedly, "C'mon out, Susie. I got a brand-new ball. My mother sent it all the way from Indian-A-polis."

Susie came as far as the porch railing and, with a note of importance in her voice, announced, "My Uncle Rob's here from Richmond to visit us. An' he says I shoultn't ever play with you anymore, Herman. Or Delores either. You're niggers!"

18

[2]

Herman was possessed by a fierce rebellion against what he considered the tiresome sameness of everyday living in Crites and by a determination to get beyond the imprisoning mountains.

"How come everything's the same all the time?" he demanded of his grandmother, not for the first time. "Can't anybody around here ever do anything different? Does every house have to be the exact same color?"

"The company paints the houses, son. They paint 'em the color they want 'em."

"Everybody goes to the same church and the same school!"

"Aren't you forgettin' there *is* only one church an' one school for us?"

"But everybody washes their clothes on the same days. Can't you pick a different day to wash our clothes, Momma?"

"Why, chile, I don' know what's the matter with you. You know why we all do the washing on Tuesdays and Thursdays. They're the only days in the whole week the mines aren't blowing out coal dust. Who's goin' to go to all the trouble of scrubbing clothes clean an' hangin' 'em on the line just so's to have coal dust blow all over them? Not me!"

19

"Well, how come the water has to be hot right at quarter to five every day, an' how come we have to have supper right at five o'clock? It makes me sick to have to do everything the same way an' at the same time every day of your life."

Hattie finished pinching the stem ends from the snap beans she was preparing for dinner and rose to her feet.

"Herman, you're a regular question box! Now you let me ask you a question. How come you get so upset about people doin' the same things in the same way? They do 'em the best way for them. The water has to be hot at quarter to five because that's when the truck brings your grandfather home from the mine. He can't eat dirty—you know that. An' when he gets through washin' up, he's tired an' hungry. So he wants his supper right away. An' that's five o'clock. There's nothin' wrong with doin' things the same way all the time if that way's comfortable for you."

The boy turned away from her, his gloom showing in his voice.

"Well, just once. Just *once* I'd like to see something different around here. Even the dumb ol' river turns black every day from nine o'clock in the morning until four o'clock in the afternoon. Why can't it turn black from eleven until seven?"

His grandmother clucked patiently. "Because they don't wash coal from eleven to seven. They wash it from nine to four," she answered with maddening calm.

The one routine Herman didn't find irritating was the butchering of the hogs, although, as with every other activity in the village, they were all butchered on the same day.

Even if he hadn't heard so much about it in the days preceding the great event, Herman thought he would have known what was coming. The men had a differ-

Christ Baptist Church, which Herman and Delores attended with their grandmother

ent air about them when they took the slops up the hillside after supper. They didn't just feed the animals and then sit around visiting—talking casually about whatever came into their heads, as they usually did. They went from pen to pen, examining each other's livestock in the manner of merchant princes comparing prize investments. Then they discussed earnestly when the execution day should be.

"I'd like to have another week, I b'lieve. I might could put another ten pound on that runt over there." That was Simon Jones, who grudged every mouthful his three scraggy hogs ate until the last few days before butchering. Then he hoped by some miracle to add instant pounds to their lean frames.

"I don' know." Harvey Overton blotted the sweat from his balding head with the blue bandanna he always carried. "Maybe we should wait on Simon. Radio says a cold spell's comin'. Better to butcher when the weather's right. Let's give Simon his week. Can't hurt the rest of us."

This year Harvey had nine to butcher—more than anyone else—and since he who had the most hogs to kill had the privilege of butchering first, Harvey's word carried weight.

By the end of the week the radio's prophecy had come true. The weather continued fair, but there was a noticeable snap in the air. And Friday evening when the men emptied the last of the pails of slop into their several pens, it was almost unanimously decided that this was the hogs' last supper. Simon Jones alone demurred. But his "I dunno—I like to have me two, three more days to fatten these fellas," was drowned in the planning of who would do what and when the next day.

Long before daylight, the almost human shrieking of the hogs wakened Herman and his sister.

"Why they scream like that?" Delores asked, shivering. "Nobody's touched 'em yet."

"They know what's comin'." Herman was pulling on his clothes. "It's only one time of year we got all the fires burnin' outside an' all the kettles heatin'. Those pigs know it. They're smart."

He crept out onto the porch. The pungent smell of wood smoke tickled his nostrils. Without stepping off the porch steps he could see ten fires burning steadily, heating the huge kettles of water. For once he was glad not to have had to man the pump. "My arms'd be clear wore off time I pumped all that water," he thought.

In the flickering firelight he could see figures moving around in the yards, adding sticks to the fires or water to the kettles. And up on the ledge men were busy catching and tying their hogs.

The executioner, revolver at the ready, strode from house to house, making sure that all was as it should be and that he knew exactly how many hogs each household had.

It would have been simpler for him to climb the hillside to the pens and shoot the hogs where they were. But to dress the carcasses in that distant spot or even to drag them down from the ledge would have cost more effort than anyone could afford.

Now, at a little after three in the morning, the bizarre parade started down the hillside toward the village, a noisily protesting hog at one end of each rope, yanking or being yanked by an unrelenting master. One by one the struggling animals were brought, each to its owner's small fenced-in yard, hauled as close as possible to the kettle simmering over the steady wood fire, and shot.

Crouched in the shadows in an angle of the fence, unnoticed by the adults who were hard at work, Herman watched the miniature massacre. One by one his grandfather's nine hogs met their executioner. One by one he shot them, quickly, neatly, and with no more feeling than he might have had about putting his heavy foot down on an ant crossing his path.

Strong arms tilted the cumbersome kettle and sloshed scalding water over the carcasses while they were still quivering. Before sunrise, busy hands were scraping the bristles from the scalded skins.

It was nine o'clock at night before the last of the animals was put away in the smokehouse. Split, and robbed of every vital part, they had hung all day in the yard spilling out their blood. The scarlet life fluid soaked into the earth making rain-defying stains. Half the winter would be gone before these signs would be erased.

Early in the day, Hattie, like her neighbors, had begun boiling the fat out of the carcasses and prepared to make soap as soon as the fat was ready.

Leaning over the porch rail at dusk, Herman surveyed the yards around him. The embers of the fires still glowed; ribbons of pungent smoke hung heavy in the air. White and glistening, the hogs hung like lost souls. They made him think of all the ghost stories he had ever heard. The air was still. No more contented grunts or peevish squeals would echo from the ledge. Not until another generation of pigs approached hoghood.

"I wish some of 'em had got away," Herman murmured aloud.

Delores, standing beside him, teased him. "You don' say a word when Momma twists an ol' hen's neck," she said. "What's the difference? The pigs an' the hens—they're both killed, and we eat 'em. *You* eat 'em too."

"I don' know," he answered dejectedly. "It just bothers me about the hogs. It bothers me bad."

And until the rains had washed away most of the blood and bristles from the dirt, he avoided the backyard as much as he could.

[3]

The possibilities of poisonous gases accumulating un-
detected far below the earth's surface or of sudden
cave-ins in the mines are constant companions of coal
miners.

Bad news travels fast in a mining town. So it wasn't
many minutes after the mine cave-in that Hattie heard
about it. She was prepared for the worst, and she prepared the children.

The only dead things Herman had ever seen were
the chickens Hattie killed for Sunday dinner, small
game—rabbits, squirrels and crows—and the hogs. He
imagined a horrid picture of his grandfather hanging
in the yard like a giant hog on butchering day.

The truck brought Harvey home, and the men carried his broken body into the house with awkward ten-
derness. When Herman, peeking out from behind the
kitchen door, saw his grandfather raise a huge hand
weakly, he was relieved and, in a curious way, disappointed.

"Shucks," he whispered to Delores, who had covered
her eyes with her hands, "he ain't dead at all. He's just
kinda sick."

Harvey wasn't dead. And he fought a mighty battle
to stave off the effects of the crushing load of slate. But

26

he lost ground steadily. On the fourth day following the accident, he died.

The night before his grandfather's burial was a living nightmare for Herman. In life this dour dark giant, his eyes permanently bloodshot from coal dust, his tread heavy and deliberate, inspired respect and some fear in his grandson and, indeed, in most who knew him. In death he lost none of his formidable power to frighten the child.

Long after those who had come to pay their respects and to sit awhile with Hattie had gone home, long after his grandmother and Delores were sound asleep, Herman lay wakeful and terrified in his narrow bed. No matter how he turned and twisted his small body, he couldn't force himself to turn away his head. He had to look through the doorway into the living room where the open coffin rested on its trestles, taking up almost the whole of the wall opposite Herman's room.

Was he really dead? Herman strained his ears to hear the least sound of breathing. What was that creaking? Was Harvey sitting up? Herman squinted into the darkness. A horrifying thought took possession of him. Were his grandfather's red eyes open, gazing sightlessly up at the stained ceiling?

This last notion became an obsession. He had to know. A dozen times his feet touched the cold floor only to be yanked back onto the bed. From sheer exhaustion the boy dozed fitfully, waking with a jerk to the same compulsion. At last, when night began to fade and the first fingers of light touched the eastern sky, he slipped cautiously off the bed. Alert and light-footed as a young fawn, and with many pauses, he forced himself to make the hundred-mile journey from his doorway to the casket. He dragged his eyes over the edge of the box, almost prepared to meet the glowing red gaze. The eyes were closed. In the half-light the child saw only a giant mask that looked vaguely like his grandfather. Teeth chattering with nerves and the chill of dawn, he skittered back through the doorway and leaped onto the bed where he fell at last into an uneasy sleep.

The slow trip to the country burying ground later in the day had meaning for him only when the lowering of the casket into the earth and the hollow sound of the clods dropping on it emphasized the trapped feeling that was the background of nearly all his days.

Herman missed his grandfather as a presence. The man's size and attitudes had commanded the esteem and approval of his peers. His wife and his grandchildren were included in the regard in which he was held. But no tears were shed at his passing. Indeed, the atmosphere of the house seemed free as it never had before. Although she didn't say so, Hattie appeared more liberated than desolated.

In later years Herman said, "My grandfather was an unusually uncommunicative man unless something irritated him. Then he spoke out loud and clear, and straight to the point. 'Close that refrigerator! Want it to frost up?' 'Shut that gate! Want the dog to get out?' were the remarks he usually addressed to me.

"My grandfather's and grandmother's life together seemed more like a business arrangement than marriage as I know it. They lived together and provided for each other, but there was no visiting between them—no small talk or exchange of ideas. Except when he was going out drinking, or she was going to church. Neither one could appreciate the other's viewpoint, and they had to bug each other about it."

His ancient hound dog, Moon, missed Harvey more than any other living creature did. There was a bond of true affection between the man and the old dog. Moon paid no attention to anyone but his master. At nineteen, nothing much moved him. A rabbit running six inches beyond his nose as he lay in the dust of the

The burial ground. Like many others, Harvey Overton's grave was unmarked

yard caused no more than a twitch of his nose and a halfhearted lifting of an ear. But he had within him a timer. About twenty minutes before five in the afternoon, he gathered his old bones together and hauled them down to the gate, arriving there just in time to greet Harvey as the latter swung in from the dirt road. The two walked up to the house together as companionably as two old men, Harvey slowing his pace to accommodate the grizzled hound's.

Moon didn't leave the house the four days Harvey lay dying. But the day after the funeral he was down at the gate at twenty minutes to five. For three weeks he kept the appointment daily, returning to the porch, restless and whining, only when night had fallen. He neither ate nor drank. Late one afternoon Herman saw Moon sprawled in the dust beside the gate, his nose between his paws, keeping his fruitless vigil.

"C'mon, Moon," the boy called. "Gran'pa's gone, an' he's not comin' back. Not ever."

The old dog gave no sign of hearing his name called. And when Herman went to get him, to lead him back to the house, he discovered that Moon had gone too.

Next morning they carried him out to the burying ground and laid him in Harvey's grave.

"Might's well let them be together," Hattie said.

(4)

Young Hattie, Herman's mother, was making a good living working in a defense plant, and she sent money home regularly to help care for her children. Charlie sent a part of his GI pay, too. Still, without Harvey's salary, there wasn't enough to take care of the needs of number 12—the little gray house and its inhabitants. When the schoolteacher couple, known as the man teacher and the woman teacher, who lived in the comfortable house high on the hillside, asked Hattie to help with the housework and look after their children, she didn't ask for time to consider the proposition. Jobs were scarce, times were hard, and the twelve dollars a week they offered were twelve dollars she needed.

His grandmother's intimacy with the house on the hill was a source of wonderment to Herman, especially since the woman teacher taught in the white school, which was next door to the colored school where Herman and his sister went.

Herman had never been inside the white school, nor did he know anyone who had been. And, although it was the biggest building he had ever seen—bigger even than the church—and its playground was fitted out with all kinds of entertaining and body-building equipment (so it seemed to Herman), he wouldn't have traded the two-room colored school with its one slide

31

The teachers lived in a comfortable house high on the hillside

The white school, in later years used by black children

and several swings for all of next-door's magnificence. Because a lazy little creek meandered through the colored-school yard, it was a source of never-ending pleasure to the children. They floated boats of twigs, leaves, bottle caps, and paper down its gentle current. They chased the long-legged bugs skidding across its glassy surface. And, squeezing the ooze of its sides and bed deliciously between fingers and toes, they made a murky mud bath of it.

White children went to the white school and were taught by white teachers. Black children went to the colored school and were taught by black teachers. It was very simple. The fact that the miners, white and black, mingled as equals at work and at the bridge had apparently nothing to do with their ideas about their children's schooling. Neither black nor white disputed separation here. To Herman it was a fact, and he wondered about it no more than he wondered why daylight should fade and night come (which he wondered about not at all).

Susie's refusal to play with him when her Richmond uncle told her she mustn't play with a black boy rested quietly in the back of his consciousness; for, shortly after her uncle returned to his home, Susie was out playing with her black friends again and accepting Delores' invitations to stay overnight at Overtons'.

It wasn't Susie and her uncle, and it wasn't school segregation itself that lighted slow-burning embers of hatred in Herman. It was the simple incident of the school bus.

A large school bus gathered the white children every morning and delivered them to their school. A small bus took the black children to their school. And this caused no comment. A large school needs a large bus. A small bus is perfectly proper for a two-room school.

But one day the small school bus broke down. The

immediate solution to the problem of getting the black children to the colored school was to take them in the white school bus. And so black and white traveled together in perfect harmony for several days until one of the miners, a white man, saw some black children getting off the bus one afternoon. Hurling himself at the startled bus driver in a blistering fury, he roared, "You been drivin' them nigger bastards in our bus? You been minglin' them with our kids? Well, you don't do it again. I'll see to that. You got no more sense than a hawg! You taken the last black animal you'll ever take in that bus. I'll see to that!"

"He did see to it," grown-up Herman later said in even tones. "And that's when I began to hate whites. It never occurred to that man that the blacks and whites were working peaceably together in the mine day after day, him included, sharing problems and helping each other. He didn't have any feeling about working there with black men. He didn't have any feeling about sitting on the bridge with black men after work, visiting with them as equals as they all washed off the day's grime in the same creek. But he didn't want his kids riding in the same school bus with niggers.

"So he called a meeting of interested parents, and the black kids never again rode to school in the white school bus. Oh, we didn't have to walk to school. It was too far away for us to walk. We got to ride in the truck that took the miners to and from the mines. I hated it. And I hated the people who made it necessary. Momma had to boil our clothes and wash them by hand. And every day the seat of my pants was black with the ground-in coal dust that lay in layers on the inside of that truck. It made extra work for Momma. The whole thing seemed senseless to me."

Looking back on the first seven years of his life still gives Herman a trapped feeling. He wasn't old enough to understand his emotions. He didn't have the experience to evaluate what was happening. But he felt closed in. He dreamed of getting past the mountain barrier that shut him away from the world.

The day-after-day sameness of Crites stifled him. The same ladies held the same conversations at the pump. Every day the kids met a half block from the bridge to talk about school or to play some games that seemed pointless to Herman. He had listened to his grandfather swinging on the same old squeaky swing evening after evening.

School was boring because he always had to wait for the kids who were too busy pinching someone or giggling to pay attention to the teacher; and no one could go ahead with the next piece of work until *everyone* was ready to move along.

All that meant security and pleasant familiarity to many children was just a dull routine to small Herman. In his immediate future he saw nothing to look forward to. He used to peer into the outside toilet to see how high the stuff was. He hoped it would fill up fast so that he could help dig a new one. That would be something to do. He wanted *two* passenger trains a day to go through town so that there would be more cars to count. He liked flowers because they grew and blossomed. Something was happening to them. They were doing something.

It was early November when Harvey Overton died. The children helped Hattie get the house ready for winter, and the cold months were spent just as they had been in other years. There was less money, but there was less strain because Hattie had a free rein in the house and the children had no sense of repression. But spring brought with it a terrifying experience. A light rain started one Saturday morning. It increased steadily during the day, and by nightfall it had grown into a relentless downpour. Herman lay awake listening to the rhythmic rattling of the raindrops against roof and windows. Then his sharp ears caught another sound. It was a hissing and a gurgling. Hattie appeared suddenly at the side of his bed, wrapped in an old coat, a scarf over her head.

"Come on, child. Get up. We got to get out of here. Looks like a flood's comin'. Get some clothes on while I get your sister up."

She melted into the darkness, and the boy, wide awake, slipped off the bed and dressed quickly. If he had any apprehension, it was brushed aside by expectation. *At last something was happening.*

Outside the house, Hattie moved as fast as she could, dragging Herman with one hand, Delores with the other, sloshing through the rising water to higher ground. Herman kept slipping, until his grandmother scooped him up and slung him around to ride piggyback. Now she could pull Delores along with a firmer grip and have one hand free to help her balance herself as well as pull her way up the slippery hillside. She didn't stop until they were a good halfway up the hill and had found a level place to rest. There they stayed, soaked and shivering, until the rain came to an end at sunrise.

Down below them the water was receding as fast as it had risen, leaving immense desolation and dismal dregs. The newly planted gardens were washed out. The tender young plants had disappeared. Small animals and chickens, dead of drowning, lay caught in the wire fencing against which they had been swept. A sore personal loss for Herman was the little white rabbit whose cozy pen had served as its trap and execution chamber.

The trio, the tall black woman with her two young charges, made their way home through mud that sucked at their feet and splashed their legs. Herman couldn't complain of boredom now. There was plenty to do. The outhouse had been washed away. A new one

36

must be built and a new hole dug. The house itself had to be swept and scrubbed to within an inch of its life. "Flood brings disease," Hattie declared. "We got to clean up." The pump was almost worn out. So were the women. So was Herman.

But some things couldn't be cleaned up. The flooding creek had stirred up and spewed out hundreds of water moccasins. And the ground had put forth thousands of worms.

"Everywhere you look they's somethin' crawlin'," Herman told Delores.

The worms died and were trampled and were disgusting. Bare feet shivered at their touch. The water moccasins were venomous and dangerous. Hattie carried her wooden mallet with her wherever she went, and the children were under strict orders not to go to the outhouse without her. Every night she lay in bed with her big flashlight beside her. When Herman or Delores had to "go out back," they roused her and she went with them, lighting the path with her flashlight, mallet at the ready. And there was seldom a night when she didn't have to kill at least one of the poisonous snakes.

Everyone's activity was drastically restricted while the plague of snakes lasted. But the atmosphere of fear and anxiety put some spice into Herman's days and nights. And he couldn't really be frightened—not with Hattie looking after him.

"Like to see any dumb ol' snake git me," he announced to Susie one afternoon when she told him reluctantly that she wasn't allowed to come down from the porch by herself until the snakes were "all kilt."

"Any ol' snake git near me or my sister, Momma goes ZAP with her mallet, an' that ol' snake got him a mashed head."

The water, though it did retreat rapidly, some sliding back into the creek, some sinking into the ground, left a few reminders of its presence: little trenches in the dirt road; new houses; replanted gardens; an alarming dearth of chickens and ducks; malodorous and scarred yards throughout the area of the company houses.

With a lazy clip-clop the community finally resumed its sluggish pace down the narrow path of habit.

[5]

One summer day a small tornado struck Hattie Overton's house. It changed the lives of Hattie and her grandchildren. It came in the person of the children's mother. Young Hattie arrived in Crites, petite, pert, and self-possessed. She arrived with a new husband, Willie Thompson, and announced that they were going to take Delores and Herman to live with them in Chester, Pennsylvania.

"We're going to take you to the city, where you can have the better things of life," Willie told Herman.

The boy couldn't remember a time when he hadn't longed to climb over the mountains; he couldn't remember a time when he hadn't yearned to leave the little mining town and become a part of the outside world. But this opportunity was so unexpected, and it came so suddenly that it gave him mental indigestion. He was eight years old, and his mind was so swollen with big ideas that his slender body could hardly support it. The internal combustion nearly tore him apart.

Who would have believed that when the day of his deliverance came Herman would try to ignore it? Who would have believed that this small black boy, who had longed all his brief life to escape from the impeding mountains and make his way into the world of happenings, would cling to his prison?

At first he was delighted. He listened with growing excitement to his mother's plans and his stepfather's descriptions. Good-by to the pump! Good-by to the tiresome sameness, the boring groove of life in Crites! Good-by to it all! Good. And, the drop of bitterness in the cup of sweetness, good-by to Momma. For she wouldn't leave her home.

"I belong here," she said firmly when Herman tried to persuade her. "What would I do in the city? Here's where my friends are. I don' know a living soul up there. Here's where my home is, Herman, and here's where I got work. [She was still working for the schoolteachers.] You go along with your mother. An' you'll be comin' back to visit, you an' Delores. It'll be like you got two houses. That one up there with your mother, an' this one here with me." Eyes that hadn't known tears even when Harvey died filled unexpectedly as Hattie said, "You'll be back for a visit real soon. Hear?"

Herman was awake before dawn. He crept to the window and watched the "Christmas tree lights" for the last time—the serpentine line of lights winking and blinking as the miners with their candle-bedecked caps wound their way up the mountainside to disappear suddenly into the mine entrance.

To enter into a new life with a mother whom he hardly remembered and a stepfather whom he knew not at all or to stay where he felt suffocated but with the person who meant most to him of anyone in the world—it was a choice almost too hard for an eight-year-old boy. But Herman had no choice to make. It was made for him. He went to Chester with his sister and the Thompsons.

Herman and Delores about the time they moved to Chester,
Pennsylvania

[6]

Herman leaned back on his elbows and let his feet hang down over the steps. He dropped his head back until his neck creaked and surveyed the Project through half-closed eyes. He could hardly believe he was really here.

The Project on Twelfth Street in Chester had been built in 1942 to house black families employed by Baldwin Locomotive Works and New York Shipbuilding. It still housed low-income black families. Its two-bedroom, living room, kitchen, and bath segments covered fifteen blocks in the city proper. Herman reflected that the whole town of Crites could have been lost in it. It was big, all right, and it included a lot of activity. However, the "better way" Willie Thompson had promised actually turned out to be an even exchange—the sameness of company houses, mining-town mores, and a trap formed by the West Virginia mountains for the sameness of low-income housing, crowded city streets, and what Herman called the track system at home.

Hattie Thompson ran a tight ship. Her small body harbored the planning skill of an admiral, the directness of a torpedo, the energy of a battleship engine. She had the determination of one who has never learned the meaning of a negative word. Her house and her family were systematized. Any deviation from what

42

she deemed proper generated instant irritation. She had never learned patience with what didn't please her. Nor had her son. But where Hattie's impatience was vocal, and had the authority of an adult, Herman's was for the most part unvoiced. He longed to be a free agent. This longing gathered strength until it became a fixed purpose, creating attitudes and actions not usual in a child of his age and background.

He began to evaluate everything that came into his experience, to make a studied judgment, and to act in accordance with that judgment. His talent for self-discipline was emerging. He wasn't always amenable to discipline imposed by others; he wasn't always obedient. But he was never openly defiant nor flagrantly rebellious. His mind was on twenty-four-hour duty, enabling him to circumvent much that he found unbearable.

The morning bathroom system was the first one he learned to beat. His stepfather invariably left the shower running, and Delores left the water running in the basin. Herman hated it. There was no sense talking about it—he had tried that once or twice. But he discovered that getting himself out of bed a half hour earlier guaranteed his having the bathroom to himself and everything to his liking.

His mother's system included certain chores for everyone. In the summer there was grass to cut; in the winter there was coal and wood to be brought in and snow to be shoveled. And all year round there were floors to be swept and scrubbed and dishes to be washed and dried. Herman did his share of the work quickly and without complaint. He liked working; it was doing something; it gave him a sense of accomplishment.

"Besides," he told Inky, his newly acquired dog, "if I do what Mother wants me to and do it right away, there's nothin' for her to bug me about."

There was something for Hattie to bug him about when Inky first arrived on the scene. Her background quite evidently and alarmingly included cocker spaniel, St. Bernard, and a number of splendid bloodlines which at the moment were a mystery. She was about to bear offspring, but what the fruit of her womb would be, no one could know until it made its appearance.

"Herman, you're not going to keep that dog! I won't have it!" was Hattie's pronouncement after one long, startled look at the animal. "It'll be messin' all over the place. And from the looks of it, it'll be havin' puppies any minute. You take it off somewhere, because you're not goin' to keep it. Hear?"

"Aw, she won't either be messin' all over," Herman replied evenly. "I guess I know how to take care of dogs. I helped look after ol' Moon, didn't I?" (He apologized to Inky silently for comparing her to nineteen-year-old Moon, who, as long as Herman had known him, had never seemed more than an animated gunnysack.) "C'mon, Mother, let me keep her. Honest, I'll clean up after her, an' you won't have any trouble with her at all. Honest."

Hattie gave him a penetrating look. "I don't think you can do it," she said at last, "but you can try." Another thought struck her. "How you goin' to feed that animal, Herman? Dog food's expensive. An' there certainly isn't enough food left over in this house to feed her an' however many puppies she's about to have!"

"I'll do it," Herman declared. "I'll figger out a way."

He made the black dog a cozy home in the coal bin, storing in bushel baskets the coal that she displaced. There she was out of his mother's way, and her messes weren't seen by the family. Since she was never allowed in the house proper, the state of her coat was of no importance to anyone but Herman, and he found her beautiful, always.

Before the puppies were born, he toyed with the idea

44

of selling them. "You have five puppies, Inky, er maybe ten, an' I can get me maybe ten, fifteen dollars for them. That'd be a nice piece of money, all right."

But as soon as he saw the blind, wriggling little morsels he changed his mind. There were seven. And he couldn't bear to get rid of one of them. As their eyes opened and they became ambulatory, staggering after one another, nudging each other in play, following Inky on rubbery legs, whimpering thin little cries, and nuzzling his gentle hands as trustingly and familiarly as they did their mother, his delight in them increased.

"Herman," his mother said, "you'll have to get rid of those pups. Now I mean it. Inky's not goin' to nurse them much longer. An' how you think you're goin' to feed eight dogs? Will you tell me that? From the looks of 'em they're part elephant. An' where you goin' to keep them? They're not comin' into the house. Don't think they are. What's more, the scraps you been collectin' for Inky aren't ever goin' to be enough to feed all of them. You better sell them, or give them away now, before you get too attached to them."

His mother's words fell on Herman's ears with sound but no meaning. Kids bored him. School bored him. People bored him. Inky and her brood were his real friends. He related to them. Taking care of them, knowing they were dependent on him, knowing they were his alone, receiving their affection and trust, gave him his first sense of personal responsibility. He tasted for the first time the sweet taste of protective love. They became the only living creatures to whom he confided freely his feelings.

"I ain't givin' 'em away, or sellin' 'em, either," he told his mother. "You see how some people treat their dogs. Nobody's gonna treat my dogs that way. I'm keepin' 'em. An' I'll feed 'em too. Don't you worry about *that.*"

Recognizing the reflection of her own immovable

will when she saw it, Hattie gave in—for the time being, at least.

"I won't worry," she replied, "as long as you feed
them and take care of them and keep them from mess-
ing up the yard. And as long as the neighbors don't
complain.

"Eight dogs!" she groaned. "I think you're crazy. An'
I'm crazy, too, for lettin' you do it."

[7]

Herman couldn't remember feeling so cheerful and alive before. Life had a purpose. He didn't want anything to foul him up at school these days. He had to get right home and look after those puppies. He went through the household chores allotted to him as a hot knife cuts through butter, because he couldn't start his real work until the assignments given him and his sister were finished to Hattie's satisfaction. He got down to the coal bin as soon as he could, cleaned up the floor, and exercised the puppies. They were growing faster than he had believed possible. And they were always hungry.

"Seems as if they inherited more St. Bernard than anything else," Herman told Inky in mingled pride and dismay. "I got to find me some way of earning money to buy food for all of you."

Characteristically, he undertook this challenge with zest and excitement. When his searching the neighborhood for odd jobs didn't turn up anything that promised a regular income, he went farther afield. One Saturday morning he discovered the Ben J. Price Meat Company at Twelfth and Engle Streets, not far from the Project. His mouth watered on behalf of his dogs when he saw the trucks leave the loading docks with their cargo of carcasses.

Armed with his need, he walked up to the dock where a man was sweeping scraps into a pile. He watched awhile. The man went on sweeping, head down, paying no attention to his audience of one.

"Need any help?" Herman stepped back to look up into the man's face. "I'm a good worker."

"I don't know what a little squirt like you can do," the man answered. He leaned on his broom and looked at Herman for the first time. "Go on inside and ask," he said. "They might have something a kid could do."

Herman followed the invisible line the man's jerking thumb drew and went into a small office just inside the huge building.

"No, thanks, sonny," the unsmiling little man behind the table answered his question. "We got enough sweepers. Tell you what, though," he added as the boy's face fell, "we could use you on the trucks. The trucks have to be scrubbed out as soon as they get back every day. How are you for being on time, hey?"

"Tell me when. I'll be here," Herman said. "How much you gonna pay?"

"Oh," the man rubbed his chin thoughtfully, "if you're any good, I guess we can pay you somewhere in the neighborhood of two dollars a week. Okay?"

Herman grinned. "That's a good neighborhood," he said. "I'll be around tomorrow. Er, how about today?"

"Come back about four," the man answered, "and you can get started."

Herman was hardly out of sight of the meat company when he had figured out an important point: Two dollars a week wasn't going to buy much dog food. His fast-growing animals were eating the best part of a can of dog food apiece, a day, besides what scraps he could wheedle from his mother. And eating was not only a habit of theirs that had to be supported, he could see that it was going to take more and more to satisfy them until they were full-grown. He didn't dare think beyond that stage.

He was back at the loading dock that afternoon long before the first trucks appeared. With the familiarity of an old and trusted employee, he entered the small office.

"I been figurin'," he told his surprised employer, "I'd rather not have the money. How about I take my pay out in scraps?"

"Wait a minute." The man sat up with a jerk. "Our meat's good government-inspected, but the scraps could be dirty, you know. We could get into trouble, maybe, lettin' you take meat home for your family. You take the two dollars, sonny. Take it or leave it."

"I don't want it for my folks," Herman explained. "You see I got these eight dogs I gotta feed, an'—"

"Eight dogs! Are you kiddin'?" The man shook his head in disbelief. "You sure you can count, kid?"

"There's eight of 'em, all right," Herman replied. "Inky's the mother. Then there's Fluffy an' Pepper an'—"

"Okay, I believe you," the man chuckled. "You can have your scraps. That is, I *think* you can. We'll see what kind of work you do before we go makin' any real promises."

The first of the trucks roared up to the dock, and Herman started working. He worked hard and happily, sweeping, scrubbing, scraping, and hosing the interior of the big meat truck. He relished activity with some point to it. When he went home for dinner he had enough scraps to feed the dogs and some left over.

"Why didn't you take the money?" Hattie asked him in amusement. "You could buy canned food and not have to mess with this junk." She looked with some distaste at the pot of simmering scraps. She sniffed, wrinkling her small well-shaped nose. "Smells good, though, I have to say that," she admitted.

"I told you." Herman was as patient as he knew how to be. "They gonna eat more an' more. The money's gonna stay the same. But if I can get all the scraps I want, I can always keep up with feedin' Inky an' the rest."

No more was said about it. It was understood by all parties concerned, even the dogs, that Herman alone was responsible for them.

Besides being the reason for meaningful after-school activity every day, Inky and her family provided a great hidden bonus. As in most inner-city areas, Chester's blocks were gang territory. It was almost impossible for a boy from first grade on up to avoid being a gang member. Herman's dogs, well-fed, strong, sleek, and healthy, were his gang. He neither needed nor wanted other companionship. They ran with him and surrounded him everywhere except at school and at work. As he had early suspected, the St. Bernard bloodline had taken the lead in their development, and they were a group to be reckoned with.

His days weren't all work and no play. There was always a ball game going on somewhere—either baseball or football—and playing ball had been a part of the youngster's life ever since he could remember. Still, when the practice or the game was over, Herman had no time to spend with the team (which was more often than not gang-oriented). He had to go to work or to go home to look after his pets.

[8]

The elementary school that Herman went to, Perry Wright, was an all-black school with an all-black faculty. The classroom work was quickly absorbed by a boy who came from a verbal and articulate family. But, as in the little school in Crites, the pinchers and the gigglers and those who couldn't find their pencils had to be accommodated. There was no opportunity for one child to move ahead alone. The class had to go on in a body or not at all. Herman practiced an air of looking and listening, but as soon as he had absorbed the current work, he blocked out teacher and classroom and went off into his own world. Or he amused himself by carrying on silent conversations with the teacher:

TEACHER: We're going to have a test next Thursday.

HERMAN: Why wait till Thursday? Let's have a test today and see what happens.

TEACHER: I want everybody to look at the blackboard. These are the problems we're going to work with today.

HERMAN: I don't want to look at the blackboard. I'm sick of the blackboard, and I know all those dumb problems backwards and forwards and upside down.

The school was terribly crowded and was finally divided into two sessions. Herman attended the first session, from 9:30 until 11:30 A.M.

Hattie didn't approve of this. "It's like you're not goin' to school at all," she said. "You're out practically all day. You got so much time to think of wrong things to do, it's hard for you to think of right things to keep busy with."

She went to school and had a long talk with the superintendent. He agreed with her that attendance at the first session left too much prime time for a youngster to get into trouble. "But the only thing I can do about it," he said, "is to let you have him come to both sessions. I wouldn't advise that with Herman, though, because he'd be so bored he'd be bound to explode in one direction or another.

"There is one thing we could do," he added thoughtfully, "we could send him to Franklin School."

The year was 1949. School integration was accepted most places in theory, if not in practice. After a great deal of discussion and a few false starts, Franklin School, an all-white school near Wallingford, Pennsylvania, on the outskirts of Chester, invited Perry Wright to send several pupils for the coming school year. Herman was one of them.

"How lucky can I get?" Herman asked Inky one afternoon when he was cleaning out the coal bin. "I get to go to Franklin."

Inky's answer was to double up and scratch one ear methodically.

"Yah, it don't mean a thing to you," Herman said. "But it's at least three miles away from here, an' I got to go on a bus. What do you think of that?"

He couldn't keep the elation out of his voice. Things were moving. Something was happening. The old track was breaking up.

His year at Franklin School had its ups and downs. If his "country" accent marked him at Perry Wright and seemed less than an advantage, certainly his color set him apart at Franklin. He and his four matching fellows from Perry Wright stood out like five blueberries in a pail of milk. In their home school they had never noticed each other. But here in alien territory they greeted each other like earth dwellers coming unexpectedly upon one another at the edge of the moon's Sea of Rains.

"It ain't that anybody's downright mean," said Jeff, a small boy with very dark skin. "It's more like we different. An' I never been around so many white people in my life before. I don' know as I like 'em very well. The kids ac' like for some reason they better 'n' what we are. An' everybody's so *pale* lookin'. It makes you feel funny," he ended lamely.

"Yeh," Herman agreed crisply. "They ain't mean. They just act like they suddenly got five chimpanzees goin' to school with 'em. They think it's kinda interestin', but they wouldn't want to make friends with a chimpanzee. Would you?"

That was about the size of it. The Chester boys moved around the school like dark shadows and with about as much effect. It probably wasn't so hard on Herman as it was on the others, because he wasn't at all dependent on school companionship. As a matter of fact, he almost had what he wanted at Franklin. More work was presented at the white school, the teachers were more demanding, classes moved faster, there wasn't the opportunity for slacking off. He had the feeling that he was getting an education. He was challenged. And if anything made him feel chipper and alive, it was the knowledge that he had to meet a challenge.

After he got used to the classroom in the basement near the furnace room ("I know how Inky feels livin' in the coal bin," he told Jeff), the first real problem he met was being asked to serve on the safety patrol.

"No, sir, I can't do it," he replied when the teacher in charge of the patrols told him he had been selected for one of the coveted positions.

"Oh, come on, boy," said Mr. Green. "You don't know what you're saying. It's an honor and a responsibility. You get to wear an armband, and you get out of your last class before everybody else."

"I know," Herman answered. "I 'preciate the honor too. But I can't do it."

He couldn't be persuaded. Nor would he say any more about it.

Soon all the teachers and most of the pupils knew that "the colored kid from Chester" had turned down safety patrol. Overnight he was classified as "rebellious" and "dumb."

Yeh, Herman thought when he heard the reaction. I'm dumb all right. I'm too dumb to want to stand on a street corner tellin' white kids in a white neighborhood they got to cross the street right here, an' they can't cross at all until I tell 'em to. He gently touched the bruise on his cheekbone, souvenir of an encounter the day before. He tried as hard as he could to avoid trouble. But a boy had accused him of tackling too hard during football on the playground.

"You niggers think you can beat on whites and win every time." The white boy looked down at Herman. "I'm gonna slap your teeth outta your black head," he promised.

"Go ahead." Herman didn't flinch. "They been slapped before."

In the fight that followed Herman was badly beaten. "Whitey got some kind of fairy tale," Herman told Jeff in the bus on the way home from school. "They got this fairy-tale idea that blacks always beat whites, an' they got to prove it different. So they're always pickin' fights."

For a while the situation worsened. Herman and the

others from Perry Wright were good moving targets for stones—small and large—refuse, and snowballs packed into hard ice balls. When they got on the school bus a short distance from the Project, they were greeted with choruses of "Old Black Joe" and original lyrics to the tune of "Cruisin' down the River on a Sunday Afternoon." One of the most repeatable of the latter blared forth, "Cruisin' in the school bus / On a Tuesday afternoon / Stoppin' by to pick up the guys / That don't belong in school."

But then one of the teachers, who had been watching Herman quietly for some time, urged him to play football with some of the groups who stayed to play every day and who were, in fact, small teams. There was a marked change in his attitude and in the attitudes of the white pupils. He was a natural ballplayer, and he loved the game. It wasn't long before he felt at home with the other players. Soon he was helping coach them, and the climate was beginning to change. The atmosphere at school so far as Herman was concerned was becoming fair and warmer.

A clincher was the annual candy sale, which the school conducted to benefit a number of worthy causes. No child was to sell outside his own neighborhood. The child who sold the most would receive a twenty-five-dollar war bond.

"I got it made," Herman boasted to Delores. "A lot of them kids live on the same block in their neighborhood. Me, I'm the only kid at Franklin that lives in the Project. I got it made!"

He was right. He sold $253 worth of candy in the Project. He had no competition. He won the war bond, and became an object of genuine interest and of some respect in the school. From then on he did very well and was reasonably happy.

When the Perry Wright boys returned to their home school at the beginning of the next school year, theirs was not a triumphant return. The news that they were back skittered around school like freakish lightning, striking in odd places and creating odd effects among students and faculty. Some couldn't have cared less whether the boys had left or whether they ever returned. Some burned with a curious and unreasoning antagonism. Others watched avidly for any idiosyncrasies that might be traced to a year's stay in a white school.

"Hey, man, looka the way he wear his hair now. Can't wear it the ol' way. Gotta show where he been last year!"

"Well, Herman, does two and two make four at Franklin? It does? Well, I guess we got nothin' to worry about. We're learnin' the same things Whitey's learnin'."

Herman seethed. Dumb, dumb, dumb! he thought. Why can't anybody get along with anybody?

(9)

Dumb, dumb, dumb! Why can't anybody get along with anybody? How come even grown-ups are always putting up roadblocks in each other's way? Even in their own way? The irritating questions with no apparent answers dominated Herman's thinking. The mechanic who lived down the block from the Thompsons didn't have a garage. He worked in the street and spilled grease all over the place. He could as easily have worked in the vacant lot at the corner where he wouldn't have bothered anyone. Half the neighborhood was up in arms about the dirt and the noise, and he was constantly on the defensive. But he wouldn't change his ways.

Herman's stepfather, Willie Thompson, always parked his car a foot or so beyond the line marking a neighbor's driveway. He and the neighbor had a running battle over it. But Willie wouldn't give in and park back the few inches that would have kept the peace.

The minister who lived directly across the street from the Thompsons had a mailbox fastened to the fence at the sidewalk. Every day he told the world (and sometimes the man himself) what he thought of a mailman so lazy he couldn't walk a few steps beyond the public sidewalk to set the mail on the porch. But he wouldn't move the mailbox itself to the porch.

"It don't make sense!" Herman told Mr. Church one day. Mr. Church, who could hardly remember his seventieth birthday, lived alone in a neat little box of a house set back from the street in a neat little patch of a yard. House and yard were as interesting to the boy as was their owner.

"Man," Herman told Inky, "it would be *somethin'* to have a house like Mr. Church's in a little yard all to yourself. We could have us a time if we could live alone with nobody to bother us, an' no track system to follow, an' no one to tell us, 'Do this, an' don't do that'!"

Mr. Church smiled his slow smile at Herman's irritation. "Now why would you want to get yourself all worked up over what other people do?" he asked. "Seems like human beings aren't happy unless they're creatin' some kind of a fuss over somethin' or other. You be like me, son. Just mind your business and let other people mind theirs. That way you keep out of trouble."

Mr. Church didn't have much business to mind—at least so far as Herman knew. The one little business he engaged in was the numbers business. Not to any great extent, it's true, but every week a certain man came around to the neat little house to take care of Mr. Church's small weekly investment. The old man never won anything.

"I'm not lucky, so far," he said to Herman one afternoon, "but some of these days Lady Luck will come ridin' in, callin' my name. You wait an' see. An' when she comes, you gonna be the first to know it."

Lady Luck did come riding in for Mr. Church, and Herman was the first to know it. She came the day that a momentous thing happened to Herman. The big fellas that played baseball down at the sandlot asked Herman to take a turn catching for them. He had gone down that afternoon, and, although some of the balls had hit his glove with what he thought was the force of a cannonball—he still wasn't absolutely sure his hand wasn't broken—he had managed to hang on to all but a couple. The fellas asked him to come back the next afternoon. He was walking on air. He had to tell someone about it besides his family. And who but Mr. Church could possibly know what the whole thing meant?

That's how Herman found out about Mr. Church's luck. He sensed it when he trotted into the little yard and saw the front door open just a crack. He heard the monotonous buzzing of flies long before he reached the steps. The stench assailed his nostrils before he reached the door.

"Mr. Church," he called. "Mr. Church, what's the—"

He never remembered pushing open the door. But he never forgot what he saw. A shotgun blast at close range is not a surgeon's scalpel. Mr. Church's luck had indeed come riding in.

Herman raced to the corner, poured out his story to the policeman he found there, ran back as far as Mr. Church's yard with the officer, and then crept around to the back of the house to vomit.

For a while after the murder the neighborhood was buffeted with waves of shock. The killer was caught and readily confessed. Mr. Church was no big-time gambler, but the numbers man had come to look upon the old man's weekly plunge as a small but sure annuity; and when, against some of the longest odds in the world, Mr. Church won, his investment officer paid him off in lethal coin.

The butchering of the hogs in Crites had distressed small Herman; his grandfather's death had frightened him; Mr. Church's murder—the first time he had ever seen a human body in violent death—made Herman sick. He never quite forgot the grisly picture. Nor was he able to stifle an emotional reaction when he passed by the little house.

It don' take long for things to fall apart, he thought. Mr. Church only been gone a month and his windows is broke, an' the grass an' weeds taken over the yard. It's like the old man never was here at all.

(10)

What Herman hoped for happened. The sandlot boys, all in their middle to late teens, put him in as a spare catcher. In his book this was the ideal position. "Man, you're right in the action when you're the catcher!" His aim was to be able to catch any kind of ball from any kind of pitcher. He would have died rather than miss practice, and he thought he was doing pretty well until the afternoon Shag, the pitcher, called out, "Okay, let's get rid of this cat an' bring on the men. I'm tired of holdin' back."

Herman was stung. He spat on his new mitt and took a firmer stance behind the plate. "What you holdin' back for?" he yelled. "Throw the ball. That's what your job is. I'll catch it. C'mon. I can catch anything you can throw. C'mon! You scared?"

Shag pulled his lips tight, and, sucking in his breath, he wound up and threw a murderous curve. If the batter hadn't ducked, he would have been beaned for sure. Herman missed the ball handily. The next two balls, if they had been straight, would have reamed a groove from Herman's fist to his shoulder.

"What the hell you tryin' to do?" howled the batter. "You tryin' to knock my head off?"

Herman crouched silently, ready for the next ball. He never opened his mouth. Once in a while he was able to catch a ball, but not often. He studied Shag's tricks and his style all afternoon, and the next afternoon, and the next. He discovered that when a ball was going to the left the pitcher leaned back a little and to the right. If he was cutting to the right, he leaned into it. A studied windup meant a ball right down the batter's shirt front. By the fourth afternoon Shag didn't have a surprise left for the tenderfoot catcher.

The rest of the team crowded around to congratulate Herman at the end of the day. He couldn't keep from grinning, but he didn't say much. He didn't take off his mitt. He was afraid his hand might come off with it. That Shag had driven in some hard ones.

"What happened to you, Shag?" he crowed like a bantam rooster. "You was fallin' down some there at the end. Your arm gettin' weak?"

The delighted cackles of the other boys didn't give him half the satisfaction that he got from Shag's baleful look.

"You sure surprised Shag." Bill Johnson slapped Herman's thin shoulders heartily. "Pretty tough on a seventeen-year-old when he can't break a little guy like you. How old are you, anyway, Herm?"

"Twelve," Herman answered. Then, paying no attention to the other boy's astonished whistle, he said, "You don' have to be so big or so old, but you gotta be able to think. Thinkin's what really matters."

And think Herman did. All the time. What he wanted most to be was the best player on the team. He never stopped thinking and planning toward that end. Most of the fellows wanted to bat first or last. Herman always wanted to bat third. That gave him two times to watch the pitcher before he came up to bat. He could figure out, then, how to act and react to the pitch.

Baseball season ended with Herman a member of the team in good standing.

In crisp weather, football was the sport, and the boy

had to earn his way there as he had in baseball. Equipment was hard to come by, and the little fellow, who was assigned to play linebacker, always seemed to get the faulty shoulder pads or the cracked helmet.

"Herman, you're crazy," his mother said, watching him touch a shoulder gingerly. "What do you want to risk getting hurt for?"

"Don't worry about this cat," he answered. "I'm thinkin'! An' I'm gonna be all right."

Just as there had been a daily baseball game after school, now there was a daily football game. The team played neighborhood teams within a wide radius. There was an excitement in moving about the city almost equal to the excitement in playing the games. But Herman always went home right after the game was over. There was a lot of horsing around and a lot of what Herman considered dumb talk. What started out as joking usually became rough and personal and, as often as not, led to fights. He steered as clear of it all as he could. He could just hear how his mother would scold if he came home with torn clothes and battle scars. But more than his mother's lectures deterred him. He knew his grandmother would be disappointed in him. Although he hadn't had a visit with her for a long time, she was still an important and very present part of his life. Sometimes he missed her so much his stomach hurt.

He knew his sister missed Momma too. But she rarely mentioned her. He and Delores didn't have much in common right now. There was love, but little communication between them. If the boys at school or in the neighborhood bothered her, Herman was always ready and willing to rescue her, but he felt no closeness to her. He translated her big-sister interest and protective attitude toward him into a kind of meddling. Sometimes she seemed more a mother than a sister close to him in age.

As far as Herman was concerned, Delores and his mother were a neat little club. He got along with them just fine, but he wasn't a member of the club.

There was no conflict between him and his stepfather. Willie Thompson had grown up in a liberal area of the Middle West and had always attended white schools. He had some very decided ideas on politeness and table manners. But, except for insisting on good manners all around, he didn't interfere with Hattie's children.

The Thompson household was not an unhappy home. If the boy in the family hadn't had such a restless fire burning in him, it might have been almost a placid home. There was always enough to eat, always enough to wear, always enough money to have a good radio and later on a television, enough to let the family go to the movies if they didn't want to go too often.

Herman's fierce sense of independence was a heritage from the two Hatties—neither of them wanted an unearned crumb; both of them enjoyed to the full knowing they were paying their way in life.

Smaller than some his age, Herman didn't have the appearance of impatience or aggressiveness. He looked rather mild. Fingernails gnawed to the quick and an occasional worrying of his lower lip with strong white teeth were the only outward signs of his inward commotion.

Unnecessary roadblocks annoyed him: the plodding at school because people didn't pay attention or because they wanted to "hack around," the neighborhood squabbles resulting from callousness to other peoples' needs, the baseball or football games lost because players goofed off or wanted to hog the limelight. These all had one label in his thinking: "Dumb roadblocks!" He decided you really couldn't depend on people. If it had been possible for him to be a team all by himself, he would have been a complete loner at this time. As it was, he conceded the necessity for working with others and set about doing so with a minimum of friction.

What he hated most was wasted effort. He wanted every thought and motion to count for something. He was constantly on the lookout for the shortest distance between two points.

With all this, Herman had a strong sense of justice. He couldn't stand a bully. Taking advantage of someone weaker, spending valuable minutes tormenting another meant frittering away useful time and energy. It was another "dumb roadblock."

He never went out of his way to correct time wasters or bullies, but whenever they entered his orbit, Herman undertook to straighten them out. Often a mutual understanding—sometimes even a friendship of sorts —followed such encounters.

For instance, there was Kenny Grant.

Kenny kept things pretty well stirred up at Perry Wright School. He wasn't a favorite with the teachers, but he managed not to come into open conflict with any of them. Large and black, with powerful long arms ending in enormous hands that became hammerlike fists at a second's notice, he was as terrifying to smaller children as a hawk to a sparrow. He appeared to have eyes in the back of his head. When any teachers were around, he toed the line like the most helpful and best of students. But when he had a chance, he tormented the younger children unmercifully.

Lunchtime gave him a wonderful opportunity. Some teachers were in their rooms at that hour; others were on duty in the lunchroom or on the playground. Usually the halls were deserted except for late-goers on their way to eat lunch. Kenny had a knack of appearing suddenly, waylaying the smaller tardy ones, relieving them of their lunch money, and slapping them around a little.

Wails and threats of "I'm gonna tell on you!" didn't

worry Kenny a bit. "You tell, an' I'll really give you a beatin'... Ain't *nothin'* gonna help you if you tell. Day you tell is gonna be the sorriest day of your life!" Thus he shut off complaints.

Kenny and his activities were an accepted part of the school day. He never bothered big kids, and the little ones didn't dare try to stand up to him. It was rumored that he carried a knife, although no one had ever actually seen it.

"Hey, Herm, got any exter money?" Jerry planted himself in front of the taller boy just inside the door of the lunchroom. "Kenny cleaned me out on the way down the hall."

"How come you let him get away with that stuff day after day?" Herman answered. "Whyn't you ever stand up to him?"

Jerry shuffled his feet impatiently. "Stand up to him, man? Who's gonna stand up to him? Answer me that! You try standin' up to Kenny, an' he knocks you down. I might be little, but I'm not dumb."

Herman's expression didn't change, but he began gnawing his lower lip—a sure sign of agitation. Absentmindedly he gave Jerry a few pieces of small change and said good-by. "See ya around."

That afternoon he waited outside of school until he saw Kenny saunter out the side door. He threaded his way quickly through little clumps of boys and girls in the school yard. When he neared Kenny he took a quarter out of his pocket and spun it high in the air, catching it neatly. "Yo, Tim," he addressed himself to an acquaintance. "Want to go to the store with me?"

Tim widened his eyes in exaggerated surprise. "What you want me to go with you for? Can't you go alone?"

Herman spun the quarter again. It was a flash of silver in the afternoon sun. "Just thought you might like some of what I'm gonna get," he answered.

66

Kenny ambled over. "I been lookin' for a quarter all day," he said. "Hand it over, son."

Herman narrowed his eyes. "It just happens I only got one quarter, Kenny, an' I need it for myself," he said softly.

"You better give it to him, Herm." Jerry was backing away cautiously.

Herman kept on walking. "I can't. I only got this one, I tell you. An' I got to keep it," he called over his shoulder.

A crowd was gathering, and Kenny played up to it. "We'll see about that," he said. "But I do hate to hit a fella littler than me."

If there was one thing Herman had learned in his couple of years playing ball with boys older and bigger than he was, it was the necessity of sizing up his opponent. He was fond of making up slogans and catch phrases to use in his frequent talks with himself. The one he had been using lately was, "Life is a think process. So keep thinkin'."

For weeks he had been sizing up Kenny. He knew exactly how the older boy operated. It wasn't Kenny's brainpower that cowed the little kids. It was his animal strength. And Herman knew from observation that when Kenny thought he had a little boy on the run, he was careless. He trusted completely in his muscle power and the other fellow's fear.

So Herman stepped up his pace. He was almost trotting. And he waited, ready for what he knew would happen. The instant the bigger boy's fist touched his cheek, Herman fell away from it, turning and planting a blow in the other's midriff.

"Whoooofff!" Kenny's breath whistled out. "I'm gonna kill you," he roared, lashing out with his heavy fists.

Herman didn't reply. He couldn't. He needed all his breath to keep dancing out of Kenny's reach. He hadn't heard of the Marquis of Queensberry. Maybe it wouldn't have made any difference to him if he had. The first chance he got, he put out a foot and tripped the big bully. Even as Kenny was falling Herman leaped on him and began pummeling him. Kenny flailed the air frantically while Herman, chin tucked well in for protection, whacked away at whatever portion of Kenny's anatomy he could reach. Twenty or thirty boys stood around cheering enthusiastically. Suddenly Herman was aware of something peculiar. Surprisingly, Kenny's furious lashing wasn't aggressive. He wasn't trying to deal Herman any blows at all. His sole effort was to ward off the younger boy and to protect himself. Abruptly Herman rolled off him and stood up. Kenny pulled himself to his feet slowly. His nose was running, and blood oozed from his upper lip. He looked uncertainly around at the audience and rubbed his face on his shirt sleeve. One of the watching small fry giggled. Someone else snickered.

"Should we try it again?" asked Herman. Kenny made a great show of tucking his torn shirttail into his pants and tying his shoelaces. Without a word he walked off. When he got to the corner, he turned once but quickly resumed his walk.

"I never knew Kenny couldn' fight," Jerry said wonderingly.

"Yeah," added Tim. "All's he can do is slap you around. An' he can't do that if you fight him. He don't even have a knife, I guess," he added with conviction. "That cat ain't gettin' none of my money anymore."

(11)

It was not dislike of people nor the desire to be alone just for the sake of being alone that kept Herman from close companionship with others. It was his constant disappointment in the human relationships he experienced. In all his life, only his grandmother had inspired his absolute respect and kindled his pure affection. He loved his mother and his sister. He liked some of his teachers. He admired many of his teammates. But he had a growing conviction that all people represented restrictions of some sort. His mother was the guard at home; she determined his comings and goings in that province. His teachers determined his actions at school. His teammates determined his opportunities on the playing field. Regardless of where he was, there was always a stop gauge with which to reckon.

Kenny Grant and his kind represented another kind of hindrance. But this kind Herman could deal with through strategy and muscle. He had no further trouble with Kenny, and to the best of his knowledge, no one else had either. Once it had been demonstrated that Kenny couldn't fight, no one feared him. His influence was over.

Sometimes, however, it seemed that the same battle had to be fought over and over in different ways at different times. Why couldn't people learn from examples? Why did the same lesson have to be taught again and again? Kenny and the boys who had watched him lose to Herman had found out what happens to bullies, but there were others who had to be shown.

Snow began falling early one November evening. It continued to fall all night. There were a good many snowball fights on the way to school the next morning, some jolly, and some not so jolly. As soon as he could, after the afternoon chores were finished, Herman took his sled to the steepest nearby hill and joined the youngsters who were coasting. Some, like Herman, had sleds. Some slid down the hill on boards, and some had big pan lids which, though freezing cold, gave their owners an exciting ride. One boy stood at the top of the hill watching the others.

"Hey, kid," he called as Herman made his way to the top for the umpteenth time. "Lemme borrow your sled. Okay? I got nothin' to ride on. I jes' wanna have one ride. I'll give it right back to you."

"Help yourself." Herman tossed him the worn rope. He watched the boy wind the rope around the middle board, run a few steps, fling himself belly down on the old sled and careen, whooping, down the icy hillside. Hands thrust deep in his pockets and shuffling his feet to fend off the cold, Herman watched his new acquaintance clamber slowly up the hill through the deeper snow beside the slick runway.

When the boy neared the top, Herman ran a few steps to meet him, holding out his hand to take the sled's rope.

The boy hardly looked at him. "Outta the way, kid," he said, shoving past the sled's owner. "I ain't through yet. I wanna have me some more rides." Turning and holding the sled high in the air, he ran a few steps to give himself a good start. Once more he hurled himself down in classic belly-flop style and rode the sled to the bottom of the crowded hill.

Herman tried to keep his eye on him, but there were so many sledders sliding down and climbing up that he lost sight of his man until he saw him flying down the steep slope again.

This time he kept a close watch and was waiting when the boy neared the top of the climb.

"All right, man," he called. "I want my sled now."

"When I'm through with it you'll be the first one to get it." The boy didn't bother to look at him. Nor did he climb clear to the top of the hill this time, but turned where he was and sailed down the slope, bawling, "Heads up!" at the top of his lungs.

Herman pursed his lips and considered the problem.

"Can I borrow your sled a minute?" he asked a nearby boy who was resting after the steep climb.

"Nah. I'm goin' down myself in a minute," was the answer.

"I don't want to slide down the hill," Herman persisted. "I'll stay right here. I just want to borrow your sled for a minute. Honest. You can watch me."

"You some kind of a nut?" asked the boy. "Well, if you just want to lean on it or something, go ahead."

Herman moved over to the crest of the hill as his sled and its hijacker approached the top. Then, grasping the back runners of his borrowed sled firmly, he lifted it above his head and brought it down on the hijacker's head and shoulders with a mighty chop.

He didn't mention the incident at home. But he wasn't altogether surprised at the storm that greeted him the second afternoon afterward when he got home from school.

"What's all this about, Herman?" His mother waved a piece of paper under his nose. "I got a bill here from a dentist. Says you did forty-five dollars' worth of damage to some kid's teeth. What have you got to say about that?"

Herman looked briefly at the bill and its accompanying note.

"All that cat had to do was gimme back my sled when I asked for it, and he could a saved all them teeth," he said mildly.

Hattie's storm blew itself out after she arranged ways for Herman to raise the money to pay the dental bill. He didn't have much free time until that bill was paid.

"People are stupid," he declared when the last of the money had been handed over. "He could a saved his teeth and saved me all the trouble if he'd a just given me back the sled that belonged to me in the first place. But no, that wasn't enough for him. He wanted me to beg for my own property. I'd rather a slid down the whole hill on my face than beg him for what was mine all the time."

"You didn't have to hit him with the sled," Hattie said reasonably.

"No, I didn't," Herman agreed. "I could a grabbed the front of the sled and stabbed him with the runners."

"Ohhh!" For once Hattie was speechless. She knew he had spoken the truth.

[12]

The Project in Chester had its drawbacks, but it began to feel like home to Herman. The smoldering resentment he harbored toward what he considered the holding game at school and at home died down as he found new ways to grow and to make use of his energy. His brief experience at Franklin School with its greater intellectual challenge made him perpetually discontented with Perry Wright, but he made a game out of outguessing teachers and fellow pupils.

It was a funny thing. Herman Wrice didn't enjoy trouble. He didn't like to fight. He didn't go looking for a fight. But somehow trouble and fights found him.

"If you think you ain't had enough," he told one burly boy who had pushed him around once too often, "we can play this whole record over again. Because I never fight the same boy a second time. We'll finish it now."

The boy didn't accept the invitation. No one ever did. He walked off with his sympathizing friends while Herman made his way home knowing in advance what his mother would say about his torn shirt, dirty trousers, and bleeding cheek.

Hattie was the dominant member of the Thompson family, and Herman avoided any confrontation with her as best he could. When the holding game, or track system, as he thought of it, became too oppressive, he quietly left the house and headed for the sizable and mysterious woods just beyond the Project. There a young boy could explore, use his imagination, and lose bristling frustrations. After a few hours of tramping along grassy paths, lying in the shadow of tall trees, listening to the hoarse cawing of the crows, he could come quietly home, refreshed and ready for the next bout.

Hattie was alert to a few of the problems confronting this impatient son of hers. She knew the traps along the road of boredom.

"Why aren't you doing your homework?" she asked one evening. "If you did your homework, you wouldn't have time to waste."

"Don't have any homework," Herman answered. "Don't have to bring home any books."

"Don't tell me that," Hattie replied sharply. "Every boy your age has homework to do. How do you expect to learn anything if you don't do what you're s'posed to do at school? You had plenty of homework and plenty of books to bring home last year."

"That was last year, and that was Franklin School," Herman said patiently. "They *give* you homework there. And you *got* to do it. Here it's just a holdin' game. They hold you in school so's you don't get into trouble outside. They don't do anything with you, but, on the other hand, they don't let you go to sleep."

"He's right, Mama," Delores broke into the conversation. "They don't give you anything to do. I don't know why, but they don't. I don't have anything to do at home, either. At least not anything that I can't do in half an hour."

Hattie's eyes narrowed. She did a quick review of the situation. Herman had never exactly lied to her, although there had been times when he had stretched the truth to give himself an advantage. He had never

74

complained about going to school. He had never hook-
ied. There had never been any bad reports come home
from his teachers. And, she thought, it was true that he
had been busy with his books during his year at Franklin School.

"Well," she said finally, "something's got to change
around here."

For Hattie to demand a change was to bring a
change about. She telephoned Mrs. Davie, with whom
she had worked in the Firestone plant in Noblesville,
Indiana, during the war. The two women were good
friends, and during the intervening years they had
kept up a warm, if desultory, correspondence. Now
Mrs. Davie was settled in Philadelphia, and once in a
while Hattie had taken the children to visit her.

"Listen, Myrtle," Herman could hear his mother
talking on the phone. "I got a problem here. I don't like
the school at all . . . No, it's nothing bad, I guess. It's just
that they don't give the kids enough work to suit me.
. . . Didn't you tell me there's a good school near you?
. . . Well, no, listen, Myrtle, I know it's a lot to ask, but
how about boarding my kids with you during the week
so that they can go to that school? I'm fed up with
things down here."

So Herman and Delores, at ages twelve and thirteen,
respectively, became boarders and commuters. For an
entire semester they lived with Mrs. Davie and went to
school—Herman to McMichael at 35th and Fairmount
Avenue and Delores to Sulzberger Junior High at 48th
and Fairmount.

Mrs. Davie was happy to have them. Her only son
had long since grown and was no longer at home; she
missed young people around her. Her house was pleasant, and the schoolwork was challenging. But Herman
was homesick. In spite of his grumblings about the
school, the teachers, the kids, and the house in the
Project in Chester, he missed them. He missed his

dogs, too. The dog family had dwindled: Several of the puppies, now grown, had died—in accidents or through illness. A couple had been lost or stolen. But Inky remained his cherished friend and companion.

Toward the middle of every week, Herman literally ached to get back to Chester. And a chronic Sunday-afternoon stomachache prefaced the train ride back to Philadelphia.

There was no use talking to his mother about his feelings. He knew that. She had meant it when she told Mrs. Davie she was fed up with Perry Wright School. Now she didn't trust any school in Chester. She had made up her mind that her children were going to have a Philadelphia School education, and that was that.

A woman at sixteen, and delivered of her second child at eighteen, she felt that she had missed something in the way of school, so she was determined to have her own children educated to the fullest of her and of their capacity.

Neither Herman nor Delores complained about lack of work in school now. There were plenty of books to take home, and there was enough homework to satisfy even Herman. He still had some deserts of boredom, but there were enough oases to make life interesting.

As he had in every school since he had begun classes in Crites, Herman began organizing a ball team. There was practice of some kind every day. And, although McMichael enjoyed the before-school, during-school, and after-school fights common to most elementary schools in an inner city, Herman was rarely involved in any of them.

He did have one significant battle early in the year. It was memorable because it scared him. He hurried out of school one afternoon and headed toward the lot where his baseball team was practicing. A slim, knobby-kneed boy approached him, leading a small band of bold ones. Herman didn't know the leader, but he had seen him at school and around the neighborhood.

"Where you think you're goin' with that bat?" asked Knobby-Knees, giving the bat a tap with his toe.

"Gonna play ball," Herman answered, attempting to shoulder his way past.

"Not unless I say so," declared Knobby-Knees.

"Now why is it," Herman asked no one in particular, "I'm always supposed to ask people to let me have things that are already mine, and beg people to let me go places where it's okay for me to go? Get outta my way, son. I'm *gonna* play ball, and I ain't gonna ask you if I can."

Like a bolt of lightning the first blow came, followed by a relentless hail. Herman fell back to get his breath. This was no powder-puff match. More than once Herman thought he heard a bone crack. One of his. Finally, after both boys had taken a sound drubbing, Herman stood over his fallen opponent.

"Okay, you want to redo this scene?" he posed his classic question. " 'Cause if you do, we'll do it right now."

Knobby-Knees shook his head to clear it and scrubbed blood mixed with tears off his face wordlessly.

"Okay, that's it." Herman grabbed his baseball bat and made an effort to walk away jauntily, ignoring, at least outwardly, his cuts and bruises. A sound made him turn his head. The other boy had gained his feet, and, followed by his gang, was starting after Herman.

"Oh, God!" Herman groaned. He clutched the bat tightly. If he comes at me again, I'm gonna have to kill him with this bat. I can't go through another fight like that. If he comes near me, I'm just gonna have to kill him, that's all.

For one electric moment the two combatants faced each other. Then, interpreting Herman's expression and the raised bat correctly, Knobby-Knees grabbed at his side. He howled a wild obscenity and, turning away, limped off.

His buddies milled around uncertainly for a minute or two then followed their leader.

Herman went on to the ball field. He ached all over. He had taken a good sound beating. That he had come out the winner was more luck than anything else, and he knew it. Now he was scared. He had known for a long time that when he played a game he wanted to be the one with CAPTAIN written on his jersey. Now he knew that when he fought, for any reason at all, he had to have WINNER on his shirt. He wanted to win badly enough to kill if he had to. He had been ready to brain Knobby-Knees with the baseball bat. It was a scary thought. During his short life, the one thing he had despised in others more than all else was failure to size up a situation and the people involved in it, failure to work things out in such a way that you could avoid trouble. "Stupid," he labeled such failure. "Dumb! Building your own roadblock!"

Now he told himself, "Herman, you gotta be careful. You gotta watch yourself real good now, or you're gonna find yourself in trouble. Bad trouble." And he put a double watch on himself to stay in control of circumstances as much as he was able, to keep his temper, to keep from being backed into mental or physical corners.

From time to time he caught glimpses of Knobby-Knees. Once in a while they came face-to-face in the neighborhood. They never became friends, but they were able to exchange curt greetings: "How you feelin'?" "Okay. How *you* been?"

The baseball team did pretty well. It moved from neighborhood to neighborhood, challenging and being challenged. They won some games and lost others. A fierce loyalty grew among the members. Practice was the most vital activity of the day. And an odd thing happened to Herman—he began to dread going back to Chester on Friday afternoons.

Now he had a group of friends in Philadelphia whom he didn't like leaving. These were boys he saw every day of the week at school and after school. His old acquaintances in Chester, whom he saw only Saturdays and Sundays, were losing their meaning for him. He couldn't be a part of their teams and games anymore, because he wasn't around enough. He was surprised to realize that a real sense of belonging in West Philadelphia possessed him.

When he mentioned, hesitantly, that he wished he didn't have to come home every weekend, Hattie was delighted. For some time she had been considering moving to Philadelphia. She, too, was beginning to yearn for a broader field of action. Delores was very happy at Sulzberger. She had made some good friends there and hated leaving them on weekends as much as Herman disliked leaving his friends. Leaving Chester for good presented no problem to her. Nor did it to Willie Thompson. He had moved his family to the eastern Pennsylvania community originally because he could work there in his brother's barber shop. But he had no fear about finding the same kind of work in Philadelphia.

So, with no one holding back, mentally or physically, the Thompson ménage moved.

(13)

The move to Philadelphia marked a new era, not only for Herman but for the whole family. They settled into 3614 Wallace Street, a comfortable house within walking distance of McMichael School. Willie found work as a barber very quickly and also began working on his own time with a jewelry firm on what was known as "Jewelers' Row" near Eighth and Sansom Streets in center city.

Hattie, who had her own very definite ideas about a mother's being at home when her children were young, decided it was all right to leave her two teenagers during the day. She found a job at a frozen-food plant at Eighth and Callowhill Streets, and everyone benefited from the added income.

Although she wasn't at home in the flesh during the day, her spirit pervaded the atmosphere. "Now look here," she advised her two children. "You can bring your friends in, but I don't want anything torn up. Hear? And you can use anything in this house. The food, the furniture, anything. We bought it. It's ours. But anything outside belongs to somebody else. You don't take anything that isn't ours. Hear?"

For Delores the rule wasn't a hard one to follow. She was interested in her girl friends and an occasional boyfriend. Most of all, she was interested in the singing that later developed into a career. Her days were filled with everything normal to almost any junior high school girl in any city in the country.

Herman, although his restlessness had stilled, lived in an atmosphere teeming with legitimate and illegitimate undertakings. He had never had so many friends in his life. The house was always filled with them.

"Where you gettin' all these kids?" Hattie asked. "Looks to me like you're bringin' the whole school home with you." But they behaved themselves pretty well, were reasonably polite to her, and didn't mess up anything. So, while she addressed them in the manner of a top sergeant, she never forbade their presence.

Who were they? They were, in effect, a gang. In the city, a forest densely planted with houses instead of trees and thickly populated, residents relate closest to the people within their own immediate area. Roughly a four-block area constitutes a home base and makes up a "family." The boys and girls in this division have a close loyalty to each other and a built-in attitude of competition with anyone from outside the neighborhood.

What is there for the young in a city to do? And where will they do it? Though Crites was a walled-in prison to a young boy, stifling in its deadly sameness, at least there had been space and growing things to watch. Though Chester had been less than interesting and demanding as far as school was concerned, it had also provided a woods to roam in and vacant lots to play in. West Philadelphia was a forest filled with action, but with very few clearings.

In the section north of Market Street where Hattie's family moved after a brief stay in the Strawberry Mansion section of North Philadelphia, having lived only a short time in the Wallace Street house, this was particularly apparent. There, in predominantly black Mantua, the numbered streets—33d, 34th, 35th, and on up to 40th—were bisected by Lancaster, Spring Garden, and Powelton. Lancaster (U.S. Route 30) was completely commercial within the city limits. Spring Garden and Powelton retained the stately single and semidetached Victorian homes built in another time for another people. At regular intervals, narrow cross streets bulged with two-story red brick houses attached to one another like a string of paper dolls. These regular rows of look-alikes bulged, in turn, with over-size families. Patches of backyards, a few of cement, a few of grass, most of well-tramped dirt, didn't provide play space adequate for other than the very young. Normal traffic made playing in the streets a hazardous adventure for older children, and casualties weren't unusual when child didn't make way for car, or vice versa. Here necessity and experience trained their involuntary pupils in a course of survival.

In these surroundings Herman Wrice ceased to be a loner in body if not in spirit. Throughout his days at McMichael and at Sulzberger, he "got along." If he wasn't an outstanding student, he wasn't a poor one. He wasn't caught up in the petty fights or midget battles erupting in school. He made his name early, and established the terms of his relationships with his peers. He had all the companionship he wanted. He had a permanent and satisfactory involvement with baseball and football. And, for the record, he wasn't absent from school a single day.

His out-of-school ventures increased their demands on him. He was by this time an important leader of the Flames from 32d Street—one of the powerful and more active neighborhood gangs. Now each day made its demands on him for convincing proof of his loyalty and ability. The team idea was dominant, as it was in all gang involvement, and most of its illegitimate operation stemmed from the need to support its legitimate pursuits.

When Herman moved there, many of Mantua's three thousand
buildings were abandoned

Baseball and football were the business of the day. Games with other neighborhood gangs were scheduled and played with as much interest as those of any professional national league. Practice was a must. And whole armies of boys marched over the 34th Street bridge to pass the Zoo and scatter for serious practice. Weekends the practice could be an all-day affair.

Proper uniforms were vital to the teams. And food was a necessity. Money was scarce—jobs were few (and if you were working at a job, you didn't have time to practice), and voluntary benefactors were nonexistent. The simplest—in fact, what seemed the only—solution was to steal what was needed. Bread trucks, lunch wagons, soft-drink trucks, and supermarkets were the victims, providing food and drink for gangs of boys who had no mental hang-ups about a direct approach to supply and demand.

They drifted in like shadows, took what they wanted, and melted away, returning to the park with the day's supplies. Parked cars provided hubcaps and other removable parts easily exchanged for money when it was needed. And the University of Pennsylvania and Drexel Institute were accessible for uniforms and parts thereof. Mantua youths, with a Robin Hood approach so far as their own needs were concerned, foiled the security guards of these two huge educational institutions with alarming ease.

Many a parent, including Hattie Thompson, reflected thankfully on the wholesome activity of sons who spent most of their time practicing and playing football or baseball or tinkering in the tiny basements of the Mantua houses. That this tinkering consisted in great part of permanently blotting out the identities of local college sports uniforms with paint and dye and filing off identifiable numbers from various stolen automotive parts never occurred to the parents.

(14)

Almost as other children in other times and in other places played cops and robbers or cowboys and Indians, plotting mock battles and scheming to swoop down on the enemy and steal away his goods, city neighborhood gangs planned and schemed and stole. They made swift forays into one another's territory, snatching water guns and ball bats at first—things they needed to play with. "It's all peewee stuff," Herman once remarked, "but you gotta do it to prove you can."

From pirating small plunder, the gangs moved on to bigger and better thievery—the baseball and football equipment and the food, mentioned earlier. There was constant pressure to prove themselves as a unit and as individuals.

"Them Counts is gettin' biggety. Got to show them who's boss around here," signaled a trip into nearby territory, resulting, if successful, in catching the Counts by surprise and giving them a good beating.

The victors strutted home to make a batch of Kool-Aid and sit around boasting, showing graphically just how they had put the whammy on the losers. "It's sickening," Herman agreed with one of the more thoughtful of his gang members, "but that's the way things are. You gotta do it. No way you can get out of it. No way."

Membership in a gang meant membership in a world where boredom was unknown. If some major activity wasn't taking place at the moment, it was being planned. A loner had no sanctuary here. Every member had a part to play in the gang's success. Personal habits, personal likes and dislikes must be forgotten. Everyone must conform—at least on the surface—to the gang's standards. Personal hates and fears within a gang were luxuries no one could afford. A strict discipline controlled members. Gang life was a way of life for even the youngest boys.

The necessity for conforming led Herman to one of the most important steps in his life. Every gang member had to have a girl to whom he could talk and boast of the gang's exploits and about whom he could talk and boast to his fellows. Herman had plenty of girl friends in school. He had girl friends in all the surrounding neighborhoods or turfs. But there was no one important girl on his own turf whom he could call his "old lady."

He didn't want just any girl. His girl had to be someone special. After all, he was a leader! Choosing the right girl was as important a decision as any he had ever been called on to make.

Just around the corner from Willie Thompson's Spring Garden Street house, on Napa Street, lived a family new to the vicinity—the Gordys. Mrs. Gordy had five children, the oldest of whom was Jean. Mrs. Gordy wasn't uppity, but she had a very real sense of obligation where her children were concerned. She worked the late shift in a drugstore luncheonette in downtown Philadelphia five days a week. Saturdays and Sundays she worked the early shift so she could have dinner at home with her family.

Most of the responsibility for taking care of the

younger children when her mother was at work fell to Jean. Although her stepfather was usually in the house, or not far away, her mother counted on Jean to be mother-in-residence to the little ones.

The Gordys had a reputation among their neighbors. They weren't allowed to run wild. They could play with other children on their street, but they couldn't wander off, and they couldn't make their house a hangout for their friends.

With their stepfather, George Gordy, a quiet, kindly man, constantly at hand, it wasn't hard to enforce Mrs. Gordy's guidelines.

"George is kind of like the invisible man," Jean told her sister Freda one afternoon when she had to urge some of the kids to get off the front steps, where they were doing what Jean called "horsing around," "but it

Gang turf in Mantua

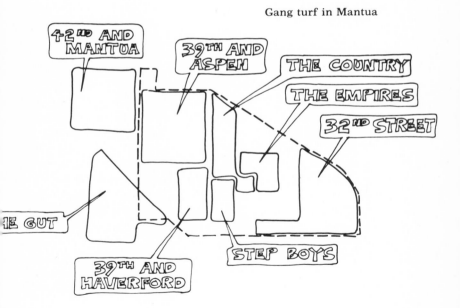

sure is handy to have everybody know there's an adult in the house. Nobody gives you any back talk."

"That Jean," the talk went, "she's somethin'. She don't hardly talk to the cats around here."

This was a slight exaggeration. She talked to them all right, but she didn't mingle with them. A little bit chubby and with slightly tilted fawnlike eyes as bright as her mind, thirteen-year-old Jean was separated by more than inclination from the children who lived around her. She went to Girls' High School on Broad Street in the city proper. Like its companion, Central High School for Boys, the school accepted from outside its geographical area only youngsters who demonstrated real ability as students.

Even while they complained about her, her peers acknowledged that there was something special about Jean. When she wasn't in school, she was on the porch steps reading, sewing, looking after her younger brothers and sister, or shepherding them on a walk or on an errand.

"Showing off," was the general criticism. "Playin' mother," some said, "so she won't have to hang out with us common ones."

Jean's mother shooed boys off the front steps and whisked her children into the house if people began loitering out front. Jean could look a person in the eye impersonally and coolly and never say a word nor answer a question if she didn't feel like it. To Herman, Jean was a challenge. This was the girl he wanted.

As he had been doing all his life when he came up against a barrier, he began the "think process." He sized up the situation. Here was a girl who wasn't an ordinary girl. She had a mother who was no ordinary mother. That mother and that girl weren't going to be interested in any ordinary cat. Well, Herman wasn't any ordinary cat. But he would have to show them, he knew. And he did.

The first step in his campaign was to lay aside his uniform of the day—soiled jeans—and appear in front of the Gordy house dressed in proper, neat, clean clothes—clean shirt, neat slacks, and shoes.

Freda, Jean's sister, was on the steps. Younger than Jean and more careless of the rules her mother laid down, she replied to Herman's question with a toss of her head and a smile. "I guess she's in the house. If she's not in school and she's not out here, I guess that's where she is. Who wants to know?"

"I do." Herman spoke politely. "Go tell her Herman Wrice wants to talk to her."

Before he could say more, the door opened, and Jean came out.

"Freda, who you talkin' to out here? Go on in the house now. Mama wants you," she added, her eyes carefully avoiding the tailor's model on the sidewalk.

"I didn't hear anyone call her," Herman said innocently.

"Oh, you didn't?" For the first time Jean looked directly at him. "Well, I guess you don't hear everything that's going on."

"I hear you." Herman moved toward the steps. "I'd like to hear more."

And that's the way it started.

When Mrs. Gordy came out the front door a little while later, she found her daughter engrossed in conversation with a freshly washed, properly dressed young man who sat on the steps as though he belonged there. She was about to explode and send him into the middle of next week, when he rose to his feet and greeted her politely.

"How do, Mrs. Gordy?" He smiled winningly. "I'm Herman Wrice. I think you know my mother, Mrs. Thompson. We live around the corner. I just stopped by to say hello."

Mrs. Gordy acknowledged the introduction and sat down on the steps.

Every little while Herman addressed a remark or a question to the watchful mother, until, her suspicion allayed, she joined naturally and comfortably in the conversation.

Herman didn't stay long that Saturday. He was his most gentlemanly self when he said good-by. But he appeared the next day and the next, always dressed properly and neatly, always polite. Before long he reached his goal.

"Come on in the house, Herman," Mrs. Gordy said one Saturday afternoon. "It's cold out here. You can come on in and sit awhile." Mrs. Gordy's acceptance of him was complete.

After that, he brought his homework to Jean's house nearly every afternoon. The two studied together. He helped Freda with her homework. He helped Jean take care of the other children and even washed the dishes sometimes when she had so much work to do that she didn't know how she could finish.

For the next several years there was no question in anyone's mind that Jean was Herman's girl. He persuaded her to make him a part of almost all her social life. The last barrier to go down before his convincing arguments was the invitation to the Girls' High Senior Prom. Herman knew exactly when it was, and he assumed he was going to take Jean. He was shocked when he brought the matter up and she told him calmly that she wasn't going with him.

"You always act like such a clown when we go anywhere," she said, "teasing everybody and making jokes and doing crazy dances. I'd be embarrassed to go with you. After all, Herman, this is a whole different bunch of people. They don't live around here. They don't know you. And I have to go to school with them. I see them every day.

"No, I don't want to go to the Prom with you. I'd rather not go at all than to go and be embarrassed."

Herman was shocked. He thought she enjoyed the broad streak of fun which his comfortable relationship with her and her family, together with his growing importance in the Flames had uncovered. He was proud of his increasing ease with people. He had thought that Jean was proud of him too.

After a long argument, which continued for the better part of a week, Jean was worn down and agreed with some misgivings to try him.

It was an elegant dance at the Sheraton, Philadelphia's newest and most up-to-date hotel. The young people looked unfamiliar in evening dress. But the strangest, the most unfamiliar of all to Jean was Herman. He was a new Herman, one she had never known before, a grown-up, sophisticated stranger. He was pleasant; he was polite; he introduced himself to the chaperones. With one ear cocked he picked up the beat of the band. "I could dance to that," he announced, and he did. He had the party spirit, and he shared it with everybody else. He charmed Jean's girl friends; he charmed her teachers; he charmed Jean. Herman-the-clown didn't put in an appearance the whole evening. Herman-the-polished-gentleman had the stage to himself.

Jean was very well aware of the envious glances darting in her direction and of the whispered comments of her school friends. She let herself be swept along as Herman, going from one group to another, joined in the conversation, telling jokes, breaking any ice that might chill the atmosphere. She loved it all.

"I had the best time," she told Herman on the way home. "I really did. I don't know what I expected. But, anyway, I had the *best time.*"

"I told you, didn't I?" he said. "I told you not to worry. Jean, you got to learn to believe what I tell you. I'm gonna be somebody sometime. An' you're gonna be somebody. We're gonna be somebody together. You better believe that!"

There were ups and downs, misunderstandings, and quarrels. Herman had girl friends in every quarter of the city and on every gang turf. If Jean went up to the field at 48th and Haverford to watch him play ball, she came home either furious or in tears because of the girl situation. Herman was always surrounded. And these were girls who belonged to his school or to the area around the playing field. Jean was always the outsider.

"I'm not going to watch the dumb games anymore," she announced bitterly one day when she had tried vainly to join Herman after a school football game. "I'm never going up there again. It gets me too upset to see them all hanging around him, and him playing the clown and grinning and encouraging them. When he wants to see me he can come see me at home!"

Freda had no such feeling. She went to the games, watched the hero-worshiping girls giggling and snuggling up to the lanky boy who seemed to be growing overnight. She watched him teasing and draping a careless arm around the shoulders of this one and that one, and on her return home she reported in vivid detail every look, gesture, and word concerning Herman. It made Jean even more miserable. Her active imagination filled in everything Freda might have omitted.

Finally Delores, who had begun to accept Jean as Herman's "real" girl, said, "Why don't you go? You got as much right to be there as anybody else. If it was me, I'd go, just to keep an eye on things."

So Jean went. She went everywhere Herman went to watch him play in school ball games, in sandlot and neighborhood games, and to watch him coach the younger boys or practice with his own teams in the park in the summertime.

Left to right: Herman's cousin Ann, Herman, his cousins Barbara and Ronnie Thompson, Delores, and Jean, ready for the dance

So long as her mother knew where she was going to be, so long as her stepfather knew that the children were all right, and so long as she took her small brothers and sister with her, she could go.

Like children playing follow-the-leader, Jean and the other girls who had little brothers and sisters to mind followed the ballplayers across the old Spring Garden Street bridge, away from the hot narrow streets of Mantua and into the grass-carpeted, tree-punctuated park.

Summer job programs for teen-agers did not yet exist. At this time, it was every man for himself. Since Herman was more than eager to earn some money, and since he couldn't stand not playing ball, he faced a real problem. But he was able to work out a solution. He interrupted the ball-playing with work as a delivery boy. He could choose his own time for working. He also bought a shoeshine kit and set himself up in business.

Shoe-shining was just the kind of business he liked. There were no limitations and no hemming in. He was the boss and the staff. If one location wasn't successful, no conference or board meeting was necessary. He picked up his office and shop and moved. His hours were his own, and they allowed plenty of time for practicing, playing ball, and gang running.

He and Jean had settled into a comfortable relationship. If she couldn't rid herself of jealousy over the twittering schoolgirls, at least she learned to live with it. In the interest of giving Herman something to think about, she made the effort to date some other boys. But she couldn't go on with that.

"Why don't you go with that Ralph anymore?" her mother asked. "You go to an all-girls school, and you don't see any fellows but Herman Wrice. You don't have any good times. You don't get to know anybody but him. You don't get out into the world at all. Now get yourself goin', Jean."

"I don't feel like it, Mama." Jean was positive. "By the time I get everything done I have to do, I honestly don't want to go out more. Besides, I don't have to go out into the world. Herman brings the world to me. He tells me what's going on everywhere. And by the time we go over all our schoolwork and his problems and find the right answers—well, the plain truth is, Mama, I don't want to go out with anyone else."

Probably no one except his grandmother knew Herman as well as Jean did. He told Jean his plans, his triumphs, and his problems. Sometimes she was just a sounding board for his own ideas. Sometimes she offered advice which he roundly criticized and pooh-poohed—and nearly always followed.

For instance, the Flames were used to crossing Spring Garden Street bridge to fight the Puerto Rican gangs who were moving into the area in increasing numbers. The battles were fought violently and often. Herman could leave one of these frays without a limp or a lump to show that he had been in the thick of things. Then he would run back to home base across the railroad trestles of the bridge.

"How can you be so dumb?" Jean asked in exasperation. "You come through the fight fine and then risk getting killed on the railroad tracks. You don't make sense."

"Don't try to tell me what to do," was Herman's irritable answer. "I can take care of myself. I been doing it a long time. Just fine."

But the next time the Flames crossed the river to fight, they all, including Herman, returned to Mantua the safe way—using the roadway and the footpath across the bridge.

(15)

Hattie, stern disciplinarian, fiercely loving, and determined regulator of her household, was never able to believe, later, that small Herman had regularly crept out of his bedroom window when they had lived in the Project in Chester. He had joined his team at night and had reentered the house noiselessly, hours later, with no one the wiser. Having once seen him safely to bed, his mother had no idea that Herman didn't stay there. Delores knew all about it, but she never told on her brother.

From whatever pool of strength, personal opinion, and sense of integrity Hattie's ideas emerged, she was always loyal to them.

"You go to school to learn," was one of her cherished ideas. "You don't go to school to act smart and get into trouble. If you get into trouble, don't come to me. I don't want to hear about it. If you get yourself into a mess, you can just get yourself out of it. I'm not going to school for you if you do wrong. Hear?"

She worked a full day. Generally, she left home before Herman left for school in the morning and returned in time to get dinner. One night, through a slip in the conversation, she learned that Herman had been home for the last three days.

"What do you think you're doing?" Hands on hips,

she faced him, sparks flying from her eyes. "You never missed a day all through grammar school and junior high. Now tell me what you're doing home from school. You're not sick. I can see that!"

Herman was uncomfortable. He was more than a foot taller than the little woman and by this time an important athlete in high school, but his mother could still make him feel like a small child caught with his hand in the sugar bowl. "Oh," he said, "this dumb teacher was bein' *real* dumb. An' I had to set him straight. He didn't like it much. An', well, they said I can't come back to school until you come up to the office with me."

"Dumb teacher!" Hattie's voice shrilled. "What makes you think he's a dumb teacher? He's smart enough to be teaching in high school, isn't he? Is that dumb? That's his job, and he's doing it. Your job is to sit there and learn what he has to teach you, not to try tellin' him how dumb he is.

"Well, you'll have to figure it out for yourself." Her voice was firm. "I told you long ago, if you get into trouble at school, don't expect me to come and patch things up for you. I can't take the time off from work to get you out of something you never should of got into in the first place. So I'm not coming to the office. Hear?"

She didn't come, either. Herman didn't really expect her to. Who knows how long he might have stayed out of school if Frances McGriff, Hattie's softhearted sister, hadn't come to the rescue. She went up to Overbrook High School with Herman, explained to the powers-that-be that his mother couldn't take off from work, and promised that Herman would walk a straight line from then on. And, except for a few minor lapses, as far as school was concerned, he didn't disappoint either Frances or Overbrook High. Certainly he didn't court suspension again.

For youth in gang-ridden cities, just crossing an

alien turf on normal business can be an enormous problem.

Sulzburger Junior High School was thirteen blocks from Herman's home, Overbrook High School was eleven blocks farther away. The girls he knew and counted as friends played an important part in Herman's safe passage from home to school and back—almost as important a part as his ball-playing, at least at first.

Sulzburger drew from a large area and included nearly a dozen turfs. There were the Tops, the Bottoms, the Main Ones, the Counts, and a number of others, including the Flames, Herman's gang, on the most eastern edge of the territory.

Every day there were incidents. That there were no murders at this time was largely due to lack of sophistication. Switchblades hadn't come into their own. Homemade zip guns, fashioned from pipes, rubber bands, and nails, were so unreliable as to make hitting a target almost a miracle. Fist fights, stompings, drubbings with sticks, pipes, or an occasional baseball bat caused considerable damage. Painful and cruel beatings left scars and disabilities that would keep the memory of these days fresh through a lifetime.

"The first thing you gotta do when you get to junior high school is make you a weapon out of some steel pipe," an experienced friend advised Herman. This was a most important, though secret, shop activity.

The mere presence of a boy on alien ground was enough to trigger an attack. No matter how a youngster came to school, on foot or by public or private transportation, there was always some point at which he had to pass through foreign territory. The chances were more than ten to one that he would be jumped as he scurried across enemy turf.

Jessie Freeman and Harold Freeman, Herman's English teacher and mechanical drawing teacher, respectively, at Sulzberger, thought and worried considerably about the student body. And both were deeply interested in Herman.

"He never seems to get involved in any of those fracases the other kids are mixed up in," Jessie said. "He never drags into school looking as if he just stepped out of a meat grinder the way so many of the others do. I'd like to know how he manages."

"I guess that's what he does," Harold answered with a grin. "Manages. I heard something mighty interesting today. It throws a little light on the subject. Remember my telling you about Sam Grissom, that big kid from the Tops who's in my ten o'clock shop?"

"The one that shoves everybody around?" asked Jessie.

"The very one. Well, here a couple months ago I was standing at a drawing board helping a kid with his blueprint when Sam let out a string of curses that would curl your hair.

"Course I had to come down on him like a ton of bricks. Got him a three-day suspension. He squawked plenty. Said a pile of books fell over on his drawing board and messed everything up. But I figured he wasn't too interested in the drawing anyway. Anything that calls for work just naturally bores him or scares him. I'd have pretended I didn't hear him—saved a lot of trouble. But Sam was just too loud to be ignored. So he had to take what was coming to him.

"Now here today I heard what really happened. Ever since school started he's been giving our friend Herman a hard time—deviling him, getting in his way, bumping into him, daring him, making trouble for him any way he can. Herman likes to play it cool, doesn't like to get pulled into a fight. But Sam was getting to him. So Herman watched his chance, evidently. He managed to knock over the books—which Sam shouldn't have had balanced on the drawing board anyway—and kill two birds with one stone: Sam had to do his drawing over, and he got a few days away from school, out of friend Herman's hair.

"The thing is, Sam doesn't know to this day how it happened. He didn't see Herman shove the books—or you can believe there'd have been one awful row. I didn't know what had happened, either."

"I guess it's wrong to laugh, but I can't help it," said Jessie. "I can't help liking Herman. He's a clown and a tease, and he has it in him to be a lot better student than he is. But he doesn't pick on anybody, and I must say, when I crack down on him he does bring in the work. I never have any real trouble with him in the academic field. And that, let me tell you, is a pleasure. How'd you hear all this?" she continued.

"Through the grapevine," her husband answered. "If and when it gets around to Sam, it might give Herman some real trouble. Well, we'll wait and see what happens."

Maybe the grapevine didn't stretch as far as Sam's ears. Or maybe he chose to ignore it. Anyway, the incident never boomeranged.

If Jessie and Harold Freeman wondered about Herman's free passage through hostile ground, Jean didn't. Baseball, football, and girls made up his passport.

Before his first term at Sulzberger was over, this boy whose obsession was baseball and football had made contact with every neighborhood team in the broad stretch from 30th Street to 59th Street. He was coaching, and he was playing with rival gangs and moving freely among them.

His friendships with girls in these territories were definitely an advantage. He had a girl friend on 35th Street, one on 41st Street, and one every few blocks all the way to school. He had girl friends in West Philadelphia, North Philadelphia, and South Philadelphia. Every one of them had an older brother who was an important member—if not the leader—of a gang.

Herman could cross any turf without fear, because he related meaningfully to at least one person of importance wherever he was. He demonstrated liking and respect, and in turn he received them.

But the Flames from 32d Street, run by "Poppy" Tate, one of the toughest and most demanding "runners" in the city, were his gang. He never lost his feeling of kinship with them, nor his appreciation of "Poppy," whom he still recalls as one of the greatest youth organizers of all times. "The guy really had talent," Herman says. "It's a shame he couldn't put it to better use."

(16)

As he grew in experience, Herman became increasingly sensitive to other people's "dumb" actions and increasingly convinced of his own ability to think his way through or around any problem. He had no fear for his personal safety, but he took on a paternal sense of obligation to everyone he thought had any claim on him. Sometimes this sense of obligation hampered constructive activity for him and for others.

Perhaps he failed to recognize his fatherly impulses because he had no father to set a pattern.

After young Hattie left him, Charlie Wrice had lived for a time in Laredo, West Virginia, a town about the size of Crites. Herman and Delores had visited him for a month or so and had had a happy enough time with him. But he remarried almost as soon as Hattie did. Now he lived in Detroit with his new wife and their son and daughter. Herman's memory of Charlie was rather vague. In spite of occasional letters from him, an effort to maintain contact, Herman rarely thought of himself as having a father.

Willie Thompson was a friendly, charming, easygoing man who kept busy with his barbering and his jewelry-making. He moved softly and quietly around the house.

"How you get along with your stepfather?" Herman was asked.

"Fine," was his answer. "I don't bother him, and he don't bother me, except for buggin' me about my table manners."

Hattie wasn't concerned about a father image for her children any more than they were. She wanted them to grow up healthy in mind and body, law-abiding, educated, and able to take their place—*make* their place if need be—in the world. A strong father image didn't seem immediately available nor important.

There were times when Herman felt this lack keenly. "When we have kids, they're gonna hate me. I know they will," he told Jean gloomily when they were discussing their future.

"What makes you talk so silly?" Jean was amused and a little bit irritated. "Why would they hate you? You're just clowning around, trying to make me tell you how great you are. You're teasing. You know our kids will probably like you a lot better than they like me."

"No, I'm not clowning," was the somber answer. "I don't know how to be a father. I never had one myself —not one I really knew."

Herman was provided with a father substitute quite suddenly and unexpectedly in the person of Sam Redding. It happened this way: Herman and Gilbert Zimmerman, a classmate and one of Herman's closest friends at Overbrook High School, were playing half-ball with a bunch of kids on Lancaster Avenue.

You play half-ball with a hard rubber ball cut in half. You throw it sideways to give it a curve, and you use a broomstick for a bat. You try to hit it up near the roof of a building. If it lands on the roof, the batter gets a home run. If it hits the wall and the pitcher catches it, it's an out. If he drops it the hitter gets a triple. A dropped ball that hits above a window is a double, and anything on the curb is a single.

There were a lot of home runs in this particular game, because the ball kept landing on the roof of the laundry in front of which they were playing. When they scrambled up on the roof to retrieve the balls, the laundry's watchman complained, and a cop appeared.

He ambled slowly across the street, giving the boys plenty of time to see him and to fade away.

"Okay," he called, as he neared the curb, "move!"

Gilbert and Herman stood their ground. The rest moved on—grumbling but moving.

"I said MOVE!" the man in blue barked.

"Aw, we're not doin' anything," Gilbert grunted.

"We're not hurtin' a thing," Herman added. "We're just playin' half-ball here. Not makin' any noise, or bustin' anything."

The cop, face reddening, walked purposefully toward the two boys. "Goddammit, I said MOVE!" His billy leaped out and smashed at the broomstick bat clutched in Herman's hand.

Automatically Herman slashed back with the broken broomstick. Automatically the cop grabbed it, and with it a handful of splinters. He glanced at his lacerated hand and started for the corner on the run.

"Riot!" he bellowed. "Riot! RIOT!"

Doors popped open, and cops poured into the area.

"Get that wise-ass over there!" The first policeman pointed to Herman, who stood beside Gilbert in the same spot where he had been standing when the blue-coat first approached. The boys gazed unbelievingly as a couple of the men in blue raced toward them. A paddy wagon pulled up. The policemen rapped the two boys sharply with their billies, roughed them up, and threw them in the police van. Booked on charges of loitering, assaulting an officer, and resisting arrest, they remained in a cell all afternoon. A crowd gath-

104

ered outside the police station, shouting and demanding the release of the two. Jean came, and a little while later Hattie appeared.

"Apologize," Jean urged Herman. "They know you weren't doing anything terrible. Just apologize, and they'll let you go."

Herman examined his bruises. "I'm not apologizing to them," he declared. "If anybody around here apologizes to anybody, they ought to apologize to Gilbert and me."

Around seven o'clock that night the turnkey came and unlocked the cell door. The two boys were taken before the desk sergeant, lectured, and let go. Neighbors and witnesses to the arrest were still standing around outside the station waiting to see what was going to happen.

Herman and Gilbert didn't have to do any talking to play hero.

The next day they were back on the same corner playing half-ball. The same policeman appeared. He walked toward them with deliberate and meaningful step.

"What are you, a couple wise-asses?" he demanded. "I told you yesterday to get away from here and stay away. Now get!"

The blood began pounding in Herman's temples, but he spoke civilly and coolly. "Do we have to go through this whole thing again, Officer?"

A short, stocky black man detached himself from a small group lounging against a building across the street. Ignoring the policeman, he addressed himself directly to Herman.

"How'd you like to play some *real* baseball?" he asked.

Herman glanced at Gilbert. "I don't mind," he said.

"Okay. You be at my house tomorrow at five. Both of you." Nodding at the two, acknowledging the policeman with a half smile, and waving a careless hand at the loungers across the street, he walked away.

The boys got to the house promptly at five the next afternoon. Sam Redding and Robert, the man who had invited them the day before, were there to greet them.

Sam was a light-skinned, thickset man of medium height, smiling and pleasant. Both Herman and Gilbert liked him the minute they saw him.

"Come on in," he said. "How about a soda?"

Over a soda and snacks Sam told them something about himself. A bachelor who had seen service overseas during the Second World War, he was a motorman on the city's elevated train line. He also owned a little bar at 54th Street and Lansdowne Avenue. His big project in life was to get a really good boys baseball team started.

Herman and Gilbert were two of the twenty-six candidates Sam finally rounded up. The boys came from assorted neighborhoods and from different gangs. Most of them were students at Overbrook High School.

Sam organized the group into a team and a family. He gave every boy a key to his house on Westminster Avenue. "There's always plenty of sodas and snacks," he told them. "I don't want you hangin' around street corners gettin' into trouble. You come on over here an' make yourself at home."

In return, Sam expected his protégés to respect his property and to keep it in good order. They all had chores to do—cleaning the house, washing windows, scrubbing paint, polishing brass, and vacuuming.

The first real assignment he gave the youngsters as a team was earning money. He sent them out to wash cars. They put their earnings into the kitty for the new Paramount Cubs—the name they picked to identify the team.

Then Sam showed them how to give a cabaret party. They filled the Imperial Ballroom at 60th and Spruce

Streets with costumed couples and singles who not only paid their way but also brought food. There was a whopping four-hundred-dollar profit from this enterprise. As fast as one project was completed, Sam figured out another one. Among other things, the Paramounts sold chance books.

At the end of two months they had over a thousand dollars in the kitty. Now Sam took them into town to a quality uniform house. With the club's earnings they bought uniforms. Not costumes, but Grade A *uniforms*. And they bought jackets, each with the owner's name embroidered on the back. Sam had the team's picture taken by a professional photographer. Pride inspired the entire group. Their whole image changed. They became known as the best-dressed team in West Philadelphia. Everything they had and everything they did was real quality. Their performance on and off the athletic field reflected this outlook.

Sam sparked in the boys pride, self-respect, and the will to achieve a desirable goal. Wishful thinking and pie-in-the-sky idealism were no part of his makeup. He was practical and enthusiastic. He demonstrated affection and respect for his boys. He gave of himself.

Soon his work was interfering with his coaching and with the game schedules for the high schoolers. He talked things over with his union boss, who, sympathetic to Sam's efforts, helped him change his work shift. Six A.M. to two P.M. working hours allowed him to be home when the boys got out of school. Now the little house on Westminster Avenue became a real center for the Paramount Cubs.

Daily practice from around two—as soon as the team could get there—until seven at night was the rule. Sam coached with a dozen or so of his friends—old buddies from the service—on hand to help. Most of the boys tried not to miss too many sessions.

"You feel like you don't want to disappoint any of

those guys," Herman told Jean. "You feel like they really care about you. For one thing, they're all puttin' five bucks in the hat every week just to keep things goin' for us. They don't have to do that, you know."

The team began making a name for itself. It called the hospital field at 46th Street and Haverford Avenue its home field, but Sam arranged games in all parts of the city and in many suburbs.

It would be hard to decide whether the boys or the community benefited more. Petty pilfering stopped as far as the Paramount Cubs were concerned, and Sam built up an interest in the neighborhood. He started the boys cleaning up the streets, working for clean block areas, being mentally and physically involved in the well-being of the turf they called home.

Eventually the whole Paramount team was made up of Overbrook High School's baseball team. They began to move smoothly and silkily, like well-oiled machinery. In the daytime they practiced and played ball at school; at night they shone as the famous and fearsome Paramounts.

(17)

Late one fall afternoon of Herman's sophomore year in high school, he and Jean sat at the old wooden table in the dining room of the Gordys' Napa Street house. The dining room was the warmest room, and it had the best light for reading.

Herman slammed shut his math book and stretched his long arms high over his head.

"Man," he sighed, "for once in my life I really got to work. Overbrook is full of white Jewish intellectual dudes, and it seems like I'm spendin' half my life just tryin' to keep up with them. You know, there's only three black kids in my bookkeeping class, an' twenty-three whites. I don' want to ask the teacher to explain things I don' understand. The white kids don' ask. I don' want it to look like this black one is the only one that's dumb. I don' mind tellin' you, though, there's plenty I don' understand right now."

Jean smiled a secret smile. Was this *Herman* admitting he was having a hard time? "That's just plain dumb," she said. "The teacher's job is to explain things. If everybody could get along without a teacher, half the colleges would close up."

"You think I want those smart cats to know I don't know something?" Herman was shocked. "You think again. I'll get it by myself if it takes me all year."

109

Doggedly he grappled with the challenge of school-work. The struggle was a new experience for him. He couldn't handle studying the way he handled "people" problems. The "think process"—figuring out how someone was going to act, and then either heading him off or changing directions before he could touch you—didn't work in book learning. He had to spend long hours in an unaccustomed activity—plain old-fash-ioned studying.

He didn't like it much, but he didn't have any choice. It was study or fail. Pride drove him, made him spend what time he needed to catch up to the "smart cats" he was competing with.

But an accident, taking any decision out of his hands, gave Herman an unexpected opportunity (although that wasn't the word he used at the time) for practically uninterrupted schoolwork. He broke his left leg during football practice. The compound fracture, complicated by serious knee and hip injuries, kept him in Philadelphia General Hospital off and on for more than eighteen months.

In traction for what seemed like half a lifetime and in almost constant pain, he was a captive student for the tutors who came regularly to keep him up to date with his class.

When he finally left the hospital, he went home a hero in a cast.

While Herman was hospitalized, his mother and Willie Thompson had separated. Hoping he would have more freedom, the boy chose to live with his step-father. Hattie wasn't at all upset. She stopped in regu-larly to be sure he was getting along all right, and he visited her often. But he couldn't hide his delight in living away from her strict rules and regulations.

"Be reasonably careful," the surgeon had warned him on releasing him from the hospital. "You've got a ways to go before you're completely out of the woods.

That hip socket was chewed up and wants a bit of looking after."

Knowing there was a pin in his hip made Herman feel sure that he would hold together. So when some of the Paramounts came by after school one day and invited him to practice with them, he didn't hesitate an instant. Being reasonably careful, he told himself firmly, didn't mean lying around the house all day.

On this red-letter day Willie had said he wouldn't be home until early evening. So Herman hobbled eagerly out of the house with his friends and was driven in style to the baseball field.

It felt good to be outdoors again. It felt great to be on the baseball field.

"I could handle a base if someone could prop me up," he told Gilbert.

"Why not?" Gilbert and a couple of others rearranged the field so first base was near the fence. They braced Herman against the fence, and the practice game was on.

Hattie decided to check on things that afternoon on her way home from work. She opened the door to bad news. Who could remember to be "reasonably careful" of a broken leg in the excitement of practice and mock games? Herman had fallen again.

The leg had to be rebroken and reset. Once more a steel pin held him together. He spent a fair amount of time in the hospital during the next two years, and, because growth in the injured leg was retarded, he gained a permanent limp and the nickname Hoppy. If either ever bothered the long, lanky teen-ager, no one knew it.

Herman was completely in love with Overbrook High School. He didn't just go to school there, he was a part of school. A key member of the football team and the baseball team during the same years that Wilt Chamberlain played basketball for the school, he also wrote for the school paper and was appointed a special guard for the locker rooms.

After that first dismal semester when he felt he was chinning the gutter, academically, Herman leaned into the challenge of schoolwork. Even the backlog of work stemming from his periods of hospitalization excited rather than depressed him.

When Jean, a year ahead of him in school, was salutatorian of her class at Girls' High, he was extravagantly proud. His own election to the senior class presidency and his positions on the teams he enjoyed most left him almost wordless.

"When I'm in anything I like to have CAPTAIN on my jacket," he reminded Hattie.

He had CAPTAIN on his jacket in school and out of school. School, gang, Paramounts, and his relations with other individuals, including Jean, were at an all-time high. It was as though he had invented perpetual motion, and every move succeeded.

His biggest problem was nighttime. "I cry when the sun goes down," he said. "Cause I have to go to bed. I'd like to live above the Arctic Circle and have a six-month day. Then I could really get things done."

Suddenly it was time for Overbrook's commencement. "Look at those dudes sittin' there," Herman told Gilbert before they started down the aisle. "All those people that never thought I'd make it. All there, seein' me graduate. Man," he went on on a different note, "I'd give a piece of my life to be able to stay here another semester. Goin' to school here was really livin'!"

Sam Redding gave his boys a graduation party with all the stops pulled out.

After the senior prom, when Sam gave the fellows money to rent tuxedoes, buy flowers for their dates, and ten dollars spending money, no one had expected anything more. But he threw a graduation party that his guests will never forget.

112

"Ask all your friends," Sam urged. "This is the big day."

"So even a lot of the white kids from Wynnefield, across the railroad bridge, are comin'," Herman told Jean. "Sam's really doin' it this time."

The whole street was alive and throbbing with rock and high spirits.

The party marked the end of an era when Herman had been able to sing the words of a song he had never sung before. The words were, "I'm here where I belong."

(18)

It was never quite clear to Herman and Delores why their father, more a name than a person to them all these years, suddenly wanted to be part of their lives again. Charlie Wrice wrote that he and his wife were living comfortably in Detroit. He wanted his firstborn children to know their half-brother and half-sister, and he was able and willing to send his two older children to college. His wife joined him in inviting them to come to Detroit to live with them.

There was discussion for and against the offer among the two Hatties and the two children, but two strong arguments sent the brother and sister to Detroit. Both mother and grandmother agreed that it was high time their father assumed a larger responsibility for these firstborn of his. And, at the moment, Charlie Wrice looked like the only hope they had of going to college. The prospect of a new experience was enough inducement for Herman and Delores.

Delores settled quickly and happily into the new life. She got along well with her stepmother and her half-brother and half-sister. Her father was proud of his beautiful daughter and showed it. Whether he was trying to make up for the past or had only lately been able to offer anything to these first children of his didn't matter. What did matter was that he was doing everything he could to give them training and opportunities they had not had before.

Delores was delighted with it all. But what was the matter with Herman? What got into him? Jean was living with relatives in New York and attending the City College of New York. She was enjoying her work as well as the change of scene. Herman was genuinely enthusiastic over her chance to go on to school and make good. But a canker of envy began festering—a "Why not me too?" feeling. He had longed for the chance to leave home and take up the challenge somewhere else.

Now he had that chance, but it wasn't nearly the prize he had anticipated. From his first day in Detroit he was at odds with his father. "Here's a man you can hate," he told his sister.

"Why? What's to hate?" Delores was honestly puzzled.

Herman couldn't give her a good answer. "He's too hip," was all he would say.

The big, dark, handsome and easygoing man, to whom Herman bore a striking resemblance, was popular with men and women, young and old. But he was never able to make a friend of his own son no matter how hard he tried. Herman kept a wall between himself and his father and never allowed a breakthrough.

Herman didn't pay much attention to his stepmother, Margaret. He treated her with outward respect, but made no pretense of being friendly with her. He couldn't, however, resist his half-brother and half-sister, who followed him like friendly puppies and were ready to do anything he asked them to do.

In the few months he lived in his father's house and attended Wayne State University, Herman was the eye of the hurricane. With great outward calm he stirred up the atmosphere, doing little or no schoolwork, smoking his father's pipes, drinking the older man's

Scotch, and leading the younger children into mischief calculated to irritate their parents.

When his father asked him to help his half-brother paint the trim on the neat little white house, Herman persuaded the willing youngster to "decorate" the entire front of the place with the bright-green paint.

The last straw for his stepmother was when he flattened a pump at the neighborhood gas station, smashing in the front of the family's new car.

"Now I've had it," the long-suffering Margaret howled. "You better *do* something with that young man, Charlie Wrice! He's been nothing but trouble since the day he came. First he made the house look like an Easter egg, and now this! I tell you, I've *had* it."

"Now, Margaret," Charlie tried to soothe her. "He's headstrong, that's all. He feels like he's got to be boss of whatever's going on. And he's got pride. He don't ever want to admit he could be wrong. I know how he is. And he's got good stuff in him.

"One reason I wanted to bring him out here is, I think a kid his age likes to feel like there's a man interested in him. And that man should be his father if that's possible. Herman's had an awful lot of women telling him what to do. I think he needs his father now."

"That's fine," his wife answered. "But what about our car? What about the damage at the gas station? That was just carelessness. Or meanness. You *know* he doesn't really like you—or me, either. And, careless or mean, it was bad!"

Charlie didn't give her a direct answer. "You know that bum leg of his gives him trouble," he said. "And he won't admit it. But I notice it stiffens up on him. I think he pulled into that gas station a little too fast, and then when he went to put on the brake he couldn't move his leg like he should. It was an accident, pure and simple. You can't blame the boy. And he's embarrassed now. Probably feels like a fool.

"We'll get a chance to talk it over one of these days when he calms down. He's keeping out of my way now, as much as he can, because he thinks I'm going to chew him out. But I'm just waiting for him to come to me. Then we can have a good talk. He's mad at himself, mad at his leg, and carrying that mad over to you and me. But we'll get a chance to straighten out the whole thing. You'll see."

Charlie may have been right about the cause of the accident. And he may have been right about Herman's feelings. But he was wrong about the talk. Herman didn't stay to talk. He left his father's house one day and didn't come back. He returned to Philadelphia.

"Well, it didn't take you long, I'll say that for you," his mother said. It was hard to tell whether she was sorry things hadn't worked out well or secretly glad that Herman hadn't established a closeness with his father. She told anyone who mentioned his name that she didn't love Charlie Wrice.

Neither did she love Willie Thompson anymore. When Herman came back, Hattie wouldn't hear of his returning to Willie's house. She insisted on his moving in with her so she could keep an eye on his activities.

(19)

As far back as he can remember there has always been some mountain Herman had to climb, or some barrier he had to break down. After he escaped the overhanging hills of Crites he had to earn a place on a ball team. He had to struggle to become team captain. He had to plot, plan, and work for the team to win games. He had to scheme so that he could move freely from turf to turf. He had to discipline himself to master his schoolwork, then compete and win in high-school politics. He had to match wits with his peers to win leadership in his gang. This was the kind of life he knew. But his return to Philadelphia from Detroit catapulted him out of the schoolboy world into outer space where goals were hazy. And he had to earn a living.

Herman had no special training, and he soon discovered that jobs—permanent jobs—were hard to find. He finally found work in a West Philadelphia lamp factory, where the work was routine. "Nothin' to it. I can do it with my eyes shut. Anybody could. I'm just puttin' in time for a paycheck," he complained.

All that kept him going now was his interest in baseball and football, which never wavered. This interest brought him back into gang life after his absence in Detroit. He went back to coaching gang teams in the park. And, because a certain amount of cash was

118

necessary to run the organization, he closed his eyes to thievery and stripping cars. He even organized crews who stole food and equipment for the teams.

Yet he resumed his relationship to Sam Redding and the Paramount Cubs. How did he reconcile his affection for Sam and his willingness to abide by Sam's inflexible rules of *no stealing, no destruction of property* with what he was doing with the Flames? Herman says that his life at this time was divided into two separate worlds. When he left one world to enter the other, he didn't look back. In Sam Redding's world he was a follower. He wanted to be like Sam, to help those who needed help, to anticipate the other fellow's need and set about supplying it. He wanted to bring fun and interesting activity into everyone's life.

In the world of the Flames he was the general of the troops. It required the daring, the self-possession, and the diplomacy of a successful general to handle the day's—and the night's—business of his troops. Herman thrived on this excitement.

Safe passage for those who wanted to visit friends in alien neighborhoods was a problem for members of lesser gangs. But the reputation of the Flames, earned through battles, planned and unplanned, coupled with the vigilance of their leader, stabilized matters for Herman's troops.

"I want to go see Lois up at 52d Street tonight," Ben might report to Herman.

"Okay." Herman would get on the phone with Dave, leader of the Tops, whose turf 52d Street was.

"Dave," he'd say, "Ben's comin' up to 52d Street tonight to see his old lady. Yeh. Lois. You know her. Now he's gonna ride up there about eight o'clock on his bicycle. And he's gonna leave about ten. Her mama don't let anybody stay there after ten, so he'll be comin' right home. He won't hang around to talk to anybody. He's comin' straight back here. So you get the word

119

around to let him in *and* out. If he's not out of there safe and sound, we'll have to come up after him. Hear?"

Dave might answer, "Okay. And one of our fellows is comin' down to see *his* old lady on 35th Street. The same thing goes for him. He'll be comin' in around seven thirty to see Maisie. He'll be leavin' by nine. Maisie's mama makes her come in plenty early. He won't poke around anywhere else. He'll go straight to Maisie's house, and he'll come straight back."

"Good," Herman might reply. "Because if we find him messin' around here at—say, ten o'clock at night, we're gonna have to make him sorry. Hear?"

This kind of daily diplomacy was routine business. Pacts were constantly being made between gangs and sometimes kept.

"Night fight on the corner of 35th and Haverford," the word would come to Herman or go to a neighborhood chief. These battles were necessary to test strength and cunning.

"No weapons," the heads would agree. "Just fists. Just punching and stomping. No weapons."

That night the "home team" would wait in the shadows outside the range of glimmering streetlamps. Experience and anticipation, like powerful drugs, set hearts racing and limbs twitching.

"Pass the pluck, man. Who's got the pluck?" a hoarse whisper would cut the silence. "Cat's gotta be crazy to get into somethin' like this without the wine to back you up."

On one such night the Flames waited uneasily for the Tops to appear. Suddenly a figure moved out of the darkness. Bill Simpson, runner for the Tops, stepped carefully into the light. Back of him shadowy figures shuffled restlessly. His men were there, waiting for a clue to their next move.

Herman approached Bill. After a few minutes' consultation they agreed that only the two leaders would fight.

The two squared off and lit into each other—fists, knees, and feet flying. The air crackled with thumps, grunts, muttered threats, and curses. Then, unable to hold back any longer, both "armies" flew at each other.

Out came the weapons—steel pipes, zip guns, knives.

A screaming police car sent both sides packing.

A few blocks away, Herman stopped to put a hand to his sweating face. His cheeks stung. In the shine of a street light he looked at his palm in disbelief. It was covered with blood. He touched his cheek again. It was dripping. The red drops fell freely, staining his sweat-shirt.

But nobody stabbed me, he thought. Nobody cut me this time. . . .

Then it came to him. The glittering gloves! That had to be it. Why would anybody wear gloves to a rumble? He remembered wondering when he first caught sight of the guy wearing them, wondering at the way they glistened when light struck them. He remembered the gloves patting at his face and his slapping them away.

He walked cautiously back to the corner. No one was there now. Only a striped cat picked its way through trash clogging an alleyway.

Herman dragged a foot along the pavement to snag any object not visible in the dimness. He stepped on something soft that crunched beneath his sneaker.

Stooping, he picked up a wad of either leather or vinyl, studded with something sharp. Trotting over to the corner, he examined his find under the streetlight. It was a glove, all right, a black vinyl glove that had been smeared with some kind of glue and dipped in shattered glass.

"Mother fucker!" Herman touched his cheek gently once again. "All that cat has to do is go around tapping a guy on the face enough times, and man, you've had it." He swore and winced when he thought what a tap on the eyes could mean.

During his years of gang-running Herman had his share of beatings. He was stabbed, cut, kicked, and stomped more than once. And he did his share of committing mayhem. He could never bring himself to shoot or stab. Punching, yes. Kicking and even stomping, yes. But the only weapon he carried was a steel pipe—the one he had made the first week he went to Sulzberger. In the night fighting it was his most trusted ally. He laid it about him with all his might. But he never waited to see its results. He didn't want to.

(20)

With Sam Redding as his model, Herman saw himself as the father image for boys who couldn't take care of themselves properly. He wanted to run anything he was involved with, because he believed he could do it better than anyone else. The one exception, so far, was Sam Redding. To him Sam Redding was king. Herman was satisfied to be crown prince. He was learning the ropes.

With his gang he was the boss. They took orders with no questions asked. Now some of Sam's affection, consideration, and sense of obligation began rubbing off on the young gang leader. He wanted his boys to follow him not only as a leader but as a friend. His feeling of responsibility for the gang members increased.

He didn't see much of Jean. She was in New York, still going to school.

She missed Herman, wondered what he was doing, and worried about him while she was out of town. But she settled into life at college and turned her attention to getting the most she could out of school. The first of her family to attend college, she was conscious of her responsibility and of her mother's extraordinary hopes for her. And wasn't she serving as an example for her younger brothers and sister at home?

Letters between her and Herman were infrequent,

but Mrs. Gordy was only too happy to report all the news to Mrs. Thompson and to Herman. In her turn, Mrs. Thompson was delighted to tell Mrs. Gordy that Herman had started taking courses at Temple University with the hope of becoming a lawyer.

Hattie Thompson didn't tell Mrs. Gordy everything Herman was doing, because there were great areas in his life at this time about which she knew nothing.

Not until years later did she understand why Herman never quarreled with her about her ten o'clock bedtime order; he went to bed willingly at the appointed hour, as old as he was. He simply stayed in his room until he was sure that his mother was settled in the living room, reading, or watching television. Then he went out of the window. He let himself down to the shed roof and from there dropped to the ground. He joined his boys and went on with whatever plans they had for the night. When the night's work or play was over, he returned to his room the same way he had left, springing up and climbing in with the agility of a cat.

His mother hadn't the slightest inkling of this while it was going on. And Herman had no sense of deceiving her. He knew from experience that he couldn't convince her of the importance of his being with his boys at night. He had heard her on more than one occasion discussing gangs and their activities with other parents.

"Herman doesn't have anything to do with that kind of business," she always said. "He goes to bed at night —early—and stays there. He's got plenty of work to keep him busy. He wouldn't have time to mess around with any of that business."

The first personal knowledge she had of his biggest interest came one spring day. Herman had begged off going to school that morning. "I'm not gonna go to school today, Mother," he said. "I got an awful headache."

"All right," his mother said, "but stay in the house. There's all kinds of sickness around. Maybe you're coming down with flu or something."

After exacting many promises from him about keeping warm, drinking plenty of liquids, and getting plenty of rest, she went off to work, satisfied that he would be all right until she got home that night.

She left work a little early and caught a bus right away. She wasn't terribly anxious about him, but she wanted to get home and make sure he was all right. Herman wasn't sick often, and he rarely complained about physical problems. When he did, she was sure something was really wrong with him.

The bus was only a few blocks from her stop and she was gazing idly out of the window when she got the shock of her life. There was Herman standing on a street corner in the middle of a crowd of boys. He was talking to them, gesturing, and they were all listening intently.

"Herman!" His mother tried desperately to open the bus window. She couldn't budge it. She hammered angrily on the glass, but no one heard her. The bus rumbled on, carrying her swiftly and inexorably past the boys, not one of whom had any idea that she was in the neighborhood or had seen them.

When she got home, seething with rage, she was ready to give Herman a large piece of her mind and a good clout on whatever portion of his anatomy she could reach first. How dared he disobey her orders and go out? Who were these boys he was with?

Six o'clock came and went. *You know you should be home for dinner.* Eight o'clock came and went. So did ten o'clock—bedtime.

Finally, about midnight, the doorbell rang. Hattie flung open the door to confront a policeman.

"You Mrs. Thompson?" he asked.

"Yes, I am."

"Well, you'll have to come down to the police station first thing tomorrow morning," said the policeman. "We picked up your son with some other boys. They were stealing hubcaps."

"Well, I won't be there in the morning, first thing or later," Hattie said positively. "I have to go to work in the morning. And that boy knows," she went on firmly, "if he gets himself into trouble, he'll have to get himself out of it.

"There's people around here go to the station house once a week to get their boys out of trouble. And those boys are *always* in trouble. If they knew their parents weren't coming to bail them out, they'd shape up.

"No, sir. I'm not taking off from work and losing a day's pay to help Herman out of something he shouldn't have got into in the first place."

She didn't go, either. And Herman hadn't expected her to.

The next day when he was called before the magistrate, who wanted to know where his mother or father was, Herman explained his mother's attitude.

Nodding approval, the magistrate questioned Herman closely, reprimanded him, and let him go.

Hattie was never able to understand Herman's reasoning about stealing the hubcaps. To her it was plain stealing, and it was wrong. To him it was simple and logical. The gangs were readying their teams for spring baseball. They had to get up a fee to play in the league. Selling hubcaps was the quickest and surest way to raise the money.

Hattie was sick about it. Her one great hope was that having to spend the night in jail would keep Herman from doing anything like that again.

When Jean received the next letter from Philadelphia, she forgot all about her family's pride in her. She came home as soon as she could pack.

"Herman needs me," was her only explanation to her disappointed mother. She couldn't be persuaded to go back to City College.

(21)

One reason Mrs. Gordy had sent Jean to New York was to separate her from Herman. She thought the two were becoming much too serious. She and Mrs. Thompson had had some minor disagreements through the years, but in this matter they saw eye to eye. Both of them had married and borne babies while still in their teens. They didn't want their children to follow this pattern.

"I love Jean," his mother told a wordless and expressionless Herman. "I always did love her ever since the first day I saw her. But I don't want you two to think of getting married just yet. You're both so young. Wait awhile. A child should stay a child as long as he can."

Mrs. Gordy backed Mrs. Thompson fervently. She couldn't hide her disappointment in Jean's refusal to go back to school nor her anxiety about her daughter's future with Herman, whom she didn't consider particularly stable.

"You both have so much growing up to do," she groaned when Jean announced that she wanted to marry Herman, and soon.

"You don't have any idea how much you'll miss if you marry now," her mother said. "First thing you know you'll have babies. How will you take care of them? How can you even take care of yourselves? With

128

Herman wanting to be a lawyer, he's got a lot of school-ing ahead of him. He won't be able to earn much of a living for a long time. You'll find yourself taking care of his house and his children and having to go out to earn money too."

Herman and Jean couldn't hear a word their parents were saying. There was a wedding. The bride and her groom were nineteen.

Herman didn't go on to school. He would not let Jean be the sole support of the family, which included a baby boy, Tobin, before their first wedding anniver-sary.

The young people were up against it. Hattie offered some help, paying for groceries and some clothing, but she was adamant about money for schooling. Herman was just as stubborn as Hattie. If she didn't want to help him on his terms, he didn't want anything from her. He went on working at a dull, poor-paying job at a laboratory and taking some courses at Temple Uni-versity. Jean found work with the Free Library of Phil-adelphia, working on a bookmobile three nights a week. They rented a room from Hattie's sister, Mrs. Frances McGriff, the same Aunt Frances who had come to Herman's rescue when he was suspended at Overbrook High School.

The McGriffs didn't have an adequate income, and although the rent they charged the Wrices was hard for the young couple to get together, it wasn't nearly enough to cover the expense of boarding them.

"Things were hard, all right," Herman says. "The house wasn't in very good shape. The wind whistled through the walls, and on winter nights Jean and I had to take the baby into bed with us to keep him warm. Even then we wondered sometimes if we'd wake up and have to knock off the icicles."

Two more babies, Terry and Tyrone, were born within the next two years. Herman was still doggedly

129

going to Temple, but he never was able to go full time. He had to make some money to feed and clothe his regularly increasing family. He had a series of jobs as cook at various restaurants and diners. In some of these places the boss appreciated his continuing at school and saw to it that he had a little time for study. But without exception there were drawbacks. The hardest problem for him was that he was always falling into the same trap: He enjoyed productive work and applied himself to it willingly—he always had— but it seemed that the more he did the more he was expected to do, with never a raise in salary. And, through pride or stubbornness, he would never ask for a raise.

The only solution he ever found for this overwork-underpay pattern was to quit the current job and look for another. Jean could never understand why he didn't come right out and say he needed more money when he was doing more work, especially since employers seemed so sorry to lose him. Several men telephoned and asked him to consider returning to work for them. His answer was always the same: "Sorry, Mr. _____, I have another job now."

"Why don't you just tell him, Herman? Tell him why you had to quit," Jean would say. "Or, anyway, tell your new boss you've got to have more money when you have to spend more time working!"

"No." Herman never went into detail. But the same situation came up time after time, and always Herman looked for a new job.

Jean continued her part-time work on the bookmobile, working from three o'clock in the afternoon until nine at night three days a week. The library appreciated her work, and every time she left to have a new baby she was welcomed back with open arms as soon as she felt strong enough to return.

She was assigned to a bookmobile in the northeast

Fourth of July, 1963. *Left to right from the top row:* Lindy, Delores'
friend; Tobin, the Wrices' first son; Herman; a grown-up Ronnie;
Terry on Grandma Hattie's lap; baby Tyrone; and Jean

section of Philadelphia, which was mainly white. At that time there was a large population of Poles and Ukrainians in the area. Black people were neither held in high regard nor, indeed, welcome. The little children knew her only as "The Book Lady," who helped them find something fun or exciting to read. They saw no difference in the color of her skin nor in the texture of her hair. But to the teen-agers she was a nigger who didn't belong where they lived. She never knew when she might be the target for their accurately aimed garbage or stones.

The librarian in charge was a Ukrainian gentleman who smarted over the harassment Jean and another black lady suffered from his neighbors.

Many an autumn or winter evening, when darkness came before the two black girls had finished working, this gallant man escorted them out of the neighborhood, walking resolutely close behind them to protect them.

One day a housewife who had brought her two young children to the bookmobile edged close to Jean. "Listen," her voice was low and earnest, "transfer out of here, why don't you, and let some nice Polish girl have your job. Nobody wants you here."

Jean returned her serious gaze. "If you know some nice Polish girl who wants this job, I wish you'd get her to apply for it."

No one did apply for the bookmobile job, and Jean stayed on until her fourth baby was born.

The babies had come regularly, one a year, Tobin, Terry, Tyrone, and now Tony.

132

[22]

About the time Mr. McGriff decided his house was too small to include his nephew's rapidly expanding family, Hattie began buying a little house on 36th Street at Fairmount Avenue. She invited Herman and Jean to move into it.

Herman still dreamed of going to law school, but the dream was fading. He had four children to support. Jean was still working part time, although she had stopped working for the library. Since she wanted to be as close to home as possible, and to cut down on her traveling time, she found a job as a tray girl at the Pennsylvania Institute, the hospital that owned the field where the Paramounts played. Her pay was small, but the food the tray girls were given to take home was a welcome aid to the Wrice budget.

Although she complained bitterly about the foolishness of people of their age and in their circumstances having four children, Hattie tried to help Herman and Jean as much as she could. She sat with the children when Jean was at work, got dinner started for them, and took the children to her house quite often. Separated permanently from Willie Thompson, she was earning her own living and trying to pay for the house on Fairmount Avenue.

Neither she nor Mrs. Gordy was able to hold back

the "I-told-you-so's" as problems mounted for their children.

Through all the ups and downs of his life, Herman clung steadfastly to playing ball. Whatever interfered with that part of his routine had to go. So when the owner of the restaurant where he was currently cooking (for ten dollars a week) asked him to work full time, Herman cheerfully stopped school to accommodate him. He got a little bit more money, but the chief advantage, as he saw it, lay in the fact that the owner allowed him to make his own schedule, and now he could take all the time he needed for ball games.

Hattie couldn't get over it.

The job didn't last too long. As had happened so many times before, the owner delegated more and more responsibility to his cook without giving him any increase in salary. Not only did the lack of money bother him, but Herman couldn't cut into his ball-playing time any further. So he quit. He talked vaguely now about going to law school "sometime." His immediate necessity was to get some kind of training so that he could earn some real money.

RCA was offering an electronics course with the promise of a job when the training was finished. Herman took the course but not the job. He went back to cooking and going to school part time. This way he could maintain the illusion of planning his own work schedule.

Tammy, baby number five, was on the way, and Mantua Hall, a high-rise housing project at 35th and Fairmount, across the street from McMichael School, was almost completed. The Wrices were tired of trying to maintain an old house. To move into this new building at a rent they could afford seemed exciting and desirable from every angle. When Jean got over worrying about the possibility of one of the children falling out of a fifteenth-story window, she agreed with Herman that Mantua Hall would be a good place to live. The protected yard with plenty of playmates for the children and having the school just across the street meant a lot to her.

Tammy's birth made some changes. Jean decided it was time to stop working outside her home except for volunteer work with scouts and school. When Herman joined Jan Pharmaceutical Laboratories as a production expediter, his regular salary met the family's needs so long as they lived at Mantua Hall. And Jean's insight told her that unless they were really in want, it was best for her husband to be his family's sole support.

"I don't know," Mrs. Gordy worried when she heard Jean's plan. "You ought to be earning *some* money for yourself. Herman hasn't stayed too long at any one job. Seems to me you should be trying to get *better* jobs instead of quitting altogether."

Jean's chin lifted and her eyelids screened her fawnlike eyes in a mannerism that always foretold one of her important statements. "Mother, in our culture the women have been keeping the men for generations. It isn't the men's fault"—her eyes were still closed—"or the women's either. But a man with a family to take care of, if he can do it, *should* be doing it. And he should know and be proud that his wife and children are counting on him. Herman can take care of us, Mother, and he wants to. And I *know* he can. Herman can do anything he says he can do." Her eyelids raised to let her calm gaze settle on her mother's troubled face. Mrs. Gordy couldn't argue with her daughter's look or words.

"I hope you're right," was all she said.

Hattie Thompson was in perfect agreement with her daughter-in-law. "A man should support his family," she declared. "A mother's place is in her home with her children, especially," she couldn't help

135

adding, "when she's got as many kids as you have." Then she lapsed into her favorite lecture: "I didn't have but two children. And you know why? Because that's all I thought I could take care of. And I was right. What do you think you're gonna do with all these kids, anyway? How you gonna take care of them? It's easy now with hand-me-downs, and they can all go barefoot. But what you gonna do later on?"

Each of Jean's pregnancies had raised her mother-in-law's eyebrows another fraction of an inch. Nevertheless, Hattie welcomed each new arrival as "Grandma's Baby," and proceeded to surround it with an almost tangible wall of love.

All the time Jean was working, Hattie had been stopping by every afternoon on her way home from her own job to make sure someone was home when the older youngsters got back from school. When Jean stayed home, Hattie stopped by daily just the same, "to be sure everything's all right with Grandma's Babies"; to play with them, take them for walks, or to give Jean a holiday by cooking supper.

Jean and Herman had a family—four active, healthy little boys and a winsome baby girl. They had enough to eat and to wear and a good place to live. They were independent. Close friends from their school days were their neighbors. The problems they were meeting—not enough room to move around in, too many children too close together, few household appliances, no car—these problems were no different from those of their friends.

Though Herman's enormous, active "thinkery" generated more energy than he could use at home, there were uses for that energy in playing ball and coaching some kind of sport every season of the year.

He threw himself more energetically into athletics. Every day was filled with activity. Any vague anxieties he had about the future he was able to sweep under the

Herman loved Jean and Jean loved children

rug with the broom of each day's necessary motion. It was a vague pain that busy hours blotted out.

He had friends and acquaintances in the four corners of the city. He could cross any gang turf as a friend. He was something of a hero to the young boys whom he trained. And although he had other interests, he maintained his gang contacts. His sense of fun worked its way to the surface, and he was becoming known as a witty fellow, sometimes a tease, always ready with some banter or a light word. This was one way he had learned to change a situation to deflect danger, to avoid unnecessary confrontations.

Above all else, he and Jean were friends. They could communicate with each other at all times. They were comfortable in each other's presence. Herman didn't know another marriage like his. "I don't know if I'm *in love* with Jean," he told a friend once, "but I really love her." He considered himself lucky not only in his marriage, but also in other areas of his life—he could always get work; he was busy; he could move freely wherever he wanted to go—but he also believed that he himself through the "think process," had been largely responsible for that luck.

He had escaped the prisoning mountains of Crites. He could go where he wanted to go, live in a decent place, do what he wanted to do—or could he? Was his larger world just a larger prison? There were times when this deeply buried thought almost surfaced.

[23]

One lazy summer afternoon Herman sat on Andy Jenkins' porch exchanging small talk. The two had been friends since grammar-school days. Their companionship included sharing through blistering heat and numbing cold the long walk to Temple University, when both were doggedly continuing their schooling.

Jean had gone to the corner store, a halfway point between the Jenkins house and Mantua Hall.

A shotgun blast split the air. The sound catapulted Herman into a new world from which he was never to return.

"There's a rumble! That came from the store!" he cried, leaping from the porch. "I saw that crazy Fred go in there a minute ago. I *thought* he was carrying something—could have been a gun," he called back to Andy, who was hard on his heels.

Feet beating the sidewalk, the young friends raced down the street. Fred burst through the store's doorway just ahead of a couple fellows Herman recognized as members of a nearby gang, and the three vanished.

Inside the little store was bedlam. Displays were overturned, cans knocked off the shelves lay in piles, and the proprietor, along with several customers, was in shock.

"Where's Jean?" Herman demanded. "She came in

here. Come on. Where is she?" Raw fear seized him.

Where was Jean? If she was all right, why wasn't she standing here with the rest of the people?

"Here I am, Herman." Quietly, and as naturally as if she had just stooped to pick up a pin from the floor, Jean rose from behind the counter.

"When I saw Fred come running in here with that gun I just dropped behind the counter."

"You could have been killed," Herman groaned, taking in the damage the shotgun had done.

"Well, I wasn't." She made a successful effort to be calm. Only a slight trembling of her hands and a rapid blinking of her eyelids gave away her fear.

"You go on home now, hear?" Herman ordered.

Jean felt the fury rising in him.

"Where you going?" she asked. "What are you going to do? Come on home with me, Herman. Listen. It's all over now. Sure it was bad. Sure, everybody could have gotten killed. I could have. But I didn't get killed. Nobody did. So come on home with me. Or go back to Andy's and forget about it.

"It's just one corner after another. It happens all the time, and you know it. I just happened to get caught in the middle. But *nobody got hurt*. Are you listening to me?"

Herman wasn't listening. He was just waiting for her to finish talking, strong white teeth worrying his lower lip in a mannerism his wife knew so well. He was planning, and nothing in the world would keep him from carrying out his plan.

"Go home like I tell you," he said, not ungently. "I'll see you."

The old leg injury that inspired the nickname Hoppy among his high-school classmates, still gave Herman some trouble. But for the most part it meant no more to him than a hangnail. Because it meant so little to him, it was soon forgotten by others. Its one

140

large effect was to cause a slight rock in his gait that made his walk seem purposeful.

Now, as he left Jean without a backward glance, he swung along Fairmount Avenue like a prizefighter coming out of his corner. His thin black eyebrows pulled his forehead into a frown. He was a six-foot-four, tenth-of-a-ton package of explosive, headed for the target.

If either of the Hatties had seen him at this moment, they would have known immediately that Herman was engaged in the "think process."

"The whole idea of the 'think process,' " he had tried to explain to Jean once, "is to figure out why people do what they do. What they think they're going to gain. And why it's so important to them to gain whatever they're after. When you know all this, you've got a chance to change things. If what they're doing bothers you, you have a chance to change the 'why,' to turn it off, maybe even keep it from happening. And if the 'why' doesn't happen, the 'what' can't happen. The 'think process' let's you cover all the angles. It keeps you away out ahead so you don't get boxed into any corners."

The fear and rage of moments ago were fading. His first impulse had been to kill somebody. He knew the gang that was involved in this shooting, and he knew where to find them.

"I figure I can get six anyway before they get me," he told himself. "That ought to give 'em something to think about."

But the "think process" began: "Yeah, an' what good's it gonna do you to kill six people? Six dead plus you. Cause you know they're gonna have to get you. Somebody keepin' score? You gonna get a prize?"

"I'm not afraid to die. I got to sometime." Herman sidestepped.

"Oh, sure," the "think process" went on. "You got to die sometime, so why not now? Is that it? But what I'm sayin' is, what good will it do anybody? That's all I'm sayin'."

Herman slowed his pace and considered. Would six or seven dead change the "why" of shoot-outs? No. It would only lead to more. It would multiply the problem.

Would his death—because there was no doubt someone would get him, if not today, then soon—make Jean proud and happy? On the contrary, it would leave her to bring up five babies alone.

He was close to his destination now. He was near the corner where the guys he was looking for hung out.

There they were, lounging against the faded brick storefront, looking as though they hadn't a care in the world. You might have thought nobody saw Herman approaching, but they all did. He knew it. He knew it because he was like them. If you wanted to survive in the world they were living in, you had to see without appearing to see and to hear without appearing to hear. You had to have eyes in the back of your head.

Careful to keep his hands away from his pockets, he came up to them. The tension was tangible. But he knew exactly what he was going to do and why.

"What do you say?" Herman's voice, steady and cordial, broke the strain. "What's everybody doin' tonight?"

There was no blood in the street; there were no broken bodies collapsed against the storefront; there was no shoot-out. There was an impromptu dinner at the Wrices. The guests were the top gang leaders of Mantua and their best men—fifteen of them—including Andy Jenkins, who had seen Jean home safely from the store earlier that fateful day.

And, like a group of executives, which in fact they were, they discussed the problems of young people in

142

Herman built up championship teams in Mantua

Mantua. This was the first time these young men had ever really talked with each other. It was the first time they had even thought of joining forces to plan something constructive for their community. They talked most of the night.

They agreed to stop fighting each other and to join in battle against their common enemy—the lack of any worthwhile opportunities in Mantua. In an atmosphere of high excitement and eagerness, they took a first step. These chief gang leaders formally united into one organization.

"Hey, man, we ought to have a name," someone said.

"Yeah," agreed another. "How's anybody going to know who we are if we don't have a name?"

"How about calling us The Young Greats?" Herman suggested the name of an old Mantua gang. "Maybe some of you remember them. They did pretty well awhile ago."

That's how The Young Great Society was born. Herman was elected president, and his long-time friend Andy Jenkins was named vice-president.

It had been a long, eventful night. As Herman stood in the doorway of his apartment saying good-by to his new associates, a surge of excitement swept over him. He loved a challenge, and what he saw ahead of him was the biggest challenge ever to confront him. Getting over the mountains surrounding Crites, surviving in the white school in Chester, making a place for himself at Overbrook High School, earning a gang leadership—all these victories shrank in significance when he compared them to wiping out gang violence in Mantua.

Closing the door with a decisive *bang,* and completely unmindful of his sleeping children, he called his wife in a voice loud and vibrant. "Jean," he called. "Come on in here, Jean. We got big things ahead of us. I want to tell you about it."

144

Afterword

This is an unfinished story of a man still in mid-career, still working on the "big things."

Time after time as we talked together, Herman made it clear to me that he was totally involved in trying to help his community, which is close to 100 percent black. He said that it was a life-and-death struggle as far as he was concerned. With a steady look and in the same tone of voice he might have used to say that there was a possibility of rain in the next few days, he told me that because of what he was doing he fully expected to be murdered.

His long-term goal is to have black people and whites learn to share their skills and work together for their common good. "But a lot of people fight this idea," he said. "They want to stay separate. And if you argue for working together, they want you out of the way. This is true about black people as well as white. There are a hundred ways my work and I could be stopped. Killing me would be the dumb way. But if some sick racist thinks that's the only way to stop me, he'll try to kill me.

"I hated white people long before it was in style," he went on. "And I got over it. Racism is a sickness. *Everybody* belongs to *some* minority group. If you get hung up on that minority business you get so full of hate you don't have much energy left for anything else. If everybody stays hung up on the minority problem, the whole nation is going to be torn apart."

As a first step in working toward having blacks and whites sharing skills and opportunities, Herman set out to make Mantua, his own community, self-respecting, self-supporting, and a pleasant, safe place to live in.

"The people of Mantua can learn to rebuild their own neighborhoods and operate their own programs," he declared.

In the beginning, The Young Great Society worked out a fairly simple athletic program for boys. Herman believed that gangs were not unlike teams and that neighborhood baseball and football teams fighting for a championship could replace neighborhood gangs fighting to wipe out each other. But he soon found out that, as in black ghettos of all cities, gang warfare was a result of poverty, unemployment, narcotics addiction, poor schools, lack of recreation facilities, and lack of decent housing.

In trying to solve these problems, The Young Great Society and its leaders started project after project: an architectural planning center, a medical center with a halfway house for narcotics addicts, a job-training center, the rehabilitation of houses that were actually falling apart, a day-care center for infants whose mothers needed to work or were going to school—all these were among the more than eighty-five projects going full swing during the two years I spent in close contact with Herman Wrice and The Young Great Society.

Within that time I saw Herman's role change from that of a leader in a small community inside a city to that of a key worker in his own city and state. I saw him become a respected consultant in many parts of this country and in Europe. Governor Shapp of Penn-

146

The Young Great Society's Building Foundation rebuilt an old wreck and made it a first-class day care center to match the artist's preview

sylvania appointed him head of a task force made up of state police, the National Guard, and a number of attorneys throughout the Commonwealth. The task force deals with civil tension and disorders, heavy drug traffic, and racial problems. It works to uncover, originate, and perpetuate jobs for young people. And it trains workers to handle all these problems.

I saw him become a meaningful part of the Human Resources Department at the University of Pennsylvania and of the Management Science Center at the same institution.

As a consultant to schools, colleges, churches, and industry, Herman avoids any kind of personal publicity. This isn't necessarily because of modesty. Rather, he's learned through some rough experiences that envy and hatred make a target of those who are successful. "They don't know how many times you've failed or how many times you've fallen," he says. "They just don't like seeing you get ahead. Also," he goes on, "the fact that I'm black would be an irritation to a lot of black people as well as to whites. They just wouldn't want me telling them what to do. It's best for me to stay in the background for everybody's sake."

There are good reasons why the complete story of Herman Wrice and The Young Great Society can't be told at this time. There are people whose lives would be in danger. There are people whose careers would be wrecked. There are important projects that would be ruined. For these reasons I've used fictitious names for some of the real-life characters.

It is still too soon to know what the real effect of The Young Great Society on Mantua will be. Many of Herman's most cherished projects have failed. And the young giant has literally sat down and cried. But there have been significantly more successes than failures. When it is possible to judge Herman and his organization in terms of what they have accomplished for their

148

community, there may have to be another book written.

"It's a twenty-four-hour-a-day job, three hundred and sixty-five days a year," he says. "And when you realize that half of every day is wasted in darkness, it's no wonder I cry when the sun goes down."

Some of the many leadership roles of Herman Wrice:

The Mayor's Outstanding Citizen of the Year 1974

    Consultant, University of Penna. Management Center (with Center's Marvin Reese)

Recipient of honorary degree in Social Science from Villanova University

    Lecturer at the University of Penna. Department of Human Resources (with Howard Mitchell, Director)

Herman Wrice

EDUCATION

Overbrook High School. Diploma, January, 1958
Temple University, B.A. 1962
Fels Institute of Local and State Government, 1965–66
University of Pennsylvania. Several undergraduate courses
Honorary degree in social science, Villanova University, 1972

EMPLOYMENT

Salesman and production expediter, Jan Pharmaceutical Laboratories, 1962–66
Consultant to the Bishop on Urban Affairs, Diocese of Pennsylvania (Episcopal) 1966 to the present
Consultant to Urban America, Washington, D.C., January, 1969
Participant in the Inner-City Seminar sponsored by Henry Ford III, 1969
Consultant to Wharton Business School, University of Pennsylvania, March, 1969
Associate Professor in Behavioral Science Department of Cheyney State College
Periodic lecturer in Black Studies at Villanova University
Consultant to Governor's Tension Task Force 1972–74

PROFESSIONAL WORK—Community Organization

1964	Organized The Young Great Society to work with gang members in the Mantua section
1965–66	Program with the Office of the District Attorney of Philadelphia County
1966–67	Organized five branch offices of The Young Great Society at the request of individuals in various communities (West Philadelphia, 2; North Philadelphia, 2; Germantown)
1967	Board member of Mantua Community Planners
1967	June—Contract with the School District of Philadelphia for summer Community Education program
1967	September—Organized Mantua Enterprises, Inc., a profit-oriented subsidary of The Young Great Society
1968	February—Formation of a community contracting business for home remodeling and vacant house rehabilitation
1968	June—Appointed Co-chairman of Philadelphia Urban Coalition. Consultant to the School Board of the City of Philadelphia. Selected for one-year membership in Black Economic Development Council
1969	Chairman of Board of Mantua Industrial Development Corporation
1969	Board member, Steering Committee, National Urban Coalition
1969	Board member, University of Pennsylvania's Community Affairs Council
1969	Board member of Citizens Council on City Planning
1969	Chairman of Board of Benjamin Banneker University
1970	Chairman of Board of Renewal Housing, Inc.
1970	Board member of Phila. Crime Commission

1970	Board member of Group Builders, Inc.
1970	Consultant to the Governor of Pennsylvania on neighborhood assistance
1971	Member of the Governor's Steering Committee on Human Services
1971	State Representative to Washington on White House Conference on Youth

THE YOUNG GREAT SOCIETY

1967	Boys Academy, 3300 Haverford Avenue
1968	Health Clinic, 603 North 33d Street
1968	Housing Office, 3301 Haverford Avenue
1969	Architecture and Planning Center, 3418–20 Brandywine
1969	Job Training Center, 614 North 33d Street
1969	Mantua Halfway House, 428 North 38th Street
1969	Mantua Academy of Theatrical Black Arts, 3302 Haverford
1969	Building Foundation Center, 4016 Pine Street
1969	Benjamin Banneker Urban University Center, 307 South 41st
1969	Infant Day Care Center, 651 North 35th Street
1969	Madcap Art Academy, 3302 Haverford Avenue
1970	Mantua Industrial Development Park, 5600 Lancaster Ave
1970	Renewal Housing, Inc., 3861 Lancaster Avenue
1970	Mantua McDevitt Scatter School Site

AWARDS

1968	United States of America Small Business Administration Award
1968	Outstanding Young Man of the Year, Philadelphia Junior Chamber of Commerce
1968	Outstanding Young Man of the Year (one of three), Penna. Junior Chamber of Commerce
1968	Philadelphia Bar Association's Citizenship Award
1968	City Teachers Association, Annual Educator Award

153

1969	Mayor's Outstanding Citizen of the Year of Philadelphia
1969	Masonic Outstanding Achievement Award
1969	Outstanding Young Man of the Year, Philadelphia Junior Chamber of Commerce
1969	The Frontiers International Outstanding Young Man of the Year of Philadelphia
1969	Frontiers International Outstanding Young Man of the Year of the nation
1969	Golden Arrow Boy Scout of America Award
1970	One of the Ten Outstanding Young Men of the Year, National Junior Chamber of Commerce
1970	Y.M.C.A. Outstanding Achievement Award
1970	Teen Center Outstanding Young Man of the Year of Philadelphia
1970	Boys Club of America Outstanding Services
1970	The Young Great Society Athletic Achievement Award
1970	Small Business Administration Award
1970	Upper Darby Junior Chamber of Commerce Award
1970	Kutztown Humanitarian Award
1970	Lancer Limited Humanitarian Award
1970	Planner Association of America Literary Award
1970	WFIL Emmy Award for YGS film documentary
1970	Unsung Hero Award for House of Ballantine
1971	Commonwealth of Pennsylvania Environmental Health Award
1971	Community Service Award, Paramount Cubs Athletic Association
1972	Commendation from Philadelphia Urban Coalition as co-chairman from 1969 to 1972
1972	Humanitarian Award from Cheyney-Mantua Summer Program
1973	Humanitarian Award from Clairton, Pa., High School Students
1974	Outstanding Volunteer Award from Mayor Frank Rizzo of Philadelphia

COMMONWEALTH OF PENNSYLVANIA

1971–72	Member of Governor's Human Services Task Force
1971–74	Member of Advisory Committee on Vocational Education
1971–	Member of Advisory Council to State Board of Public Welfare
1971–	Consultant to Governor's Committee on Civil Tensions

Acknowledgments

I owe thanks to many people for the material in this book: Herman and Jean Wrice; Hattie Thompson and Charlie Wrice—Herman's mother and father; Delores, Herman's sister; Edith McGriff, his aunt; Bill Ellson; Gene Hoke; Tom Gallagher; Jessie and Harold Freeman, Herman's teachers; Russell Ackoff, Director of Busch Center, University of Pennsylvania; Marvin Reese, Assistant to the Director of the Busch Center, University of Pennsylvania; Howard Mitchell of the University of Pennsylvania Human Resources Center; Webster Christman; Bill Sturgis; Charles Calloway; Father Clayton Hewitt; the Right Reverend Robert L. DeWitt, former Episcopal Bishop of Pennsylvania; Dr. Ruth Hayre, Superintendent of District IV in the Philadelphia School System; Dr. Wade Wilson, President of Cheyney State College. All of these I know by name. But there were many more—Mantuans young and old —whom I met casually on the streets of their community and who shared their feelings about Herman with me.

A special thanks is due also to the attendants in the morgue of the Philadelphia Evening Bulletin.

156

Index

157